AS IF BY MAGIC

First published in 2020 by
The Dedalus Press
13 Moyclare Road
Baldoyle
Dublin D13 K1C2
Ireland

www.dedaluspress.com

ISBN 9781910251775 (paperback)
ISBN 9781910251782 (hardback)

Dedalus Press titles are available in Ireland
from Argosy Books (www.argosybooks.ie) and in the UK
from Inpress Books (www.inpressbooks.co.uk)

Cover image: Paula Meehan

The Dedalus Press receives financial assistance from
The Arts Council / An Chomhairle Ealaíon.

AS IF BY MAGIC
SELECTED POEMS

PAULA MEEHAN

DEDALUS PRESS

Contents

from **Dharmakaya** (2000)

from **Geomantic** (2016)

For my sisters Lola Beatty, Brenda Doyle, Antoinette Milne,
for my brother Martin Meehan,

&

in memory Paula and Alan McCarthy

ACKNOWLEDGEMENTS

The Dedalus Press acknowledges and is grateful to Carcanet Press for permission to include poems from Paula Meehan's two Carcanet collections, *Dharmakaya* (2000) and *Painting Rain* (2009), in the preparation of this volume.

from

The Man Who Was Marked By Winter

(1991)

for Tony Cafferky

The Leaving

He had fallen so far down into himself
I couldn't reach him.
Though I had arranged our escape
he wouldn't budge. He sat
days in his room checking manuscripts

or fixing photos of his family
strictly in the order they were taken.
I begged him hurry for
the moonless nights were due;
it was two nights' walk through the forest.

The soldiers had recently entered our quarter.
I dreaded each knock on the door,
their heavy boots on the stairs.
Our friends advised haste;
many neighbours were already in prison.

His eyes were twin suns burning.
Silence was his answer to my pleas.
I packed a change of clothes, half
the remaining rations,
my mother's gold ring for barter.

The documents at a glance would pass.
It wasn't for myself I went but
for the new life I carried.
At the frontier I recalled him — that last morning
by the window watching the sun

strut the length of the street, mirroring
the clouds' parade. He wore

the black shirt I'd embroidered with stars
and said nothing. Nothing.
Then the guide pushed me forward.

Between one sweep of the searchlight
and the next, I slipped into another state
gratefully, under cover of darkness.

Her Dream

This is the fountain. You could overlook it
from a balcony. I would cup
cool water under the moon's reflection
occluding the lines on my palm.

I would carry this small moon for you
through the city's narrow streets, through
blighted raging days to fling it at your feet:
a spent coin thrown down on cobbles.

I would wear a white dress edged with poppies,
I would pin golden rings in my ears
and walk the rim of the fountain round
to spin you a fatal story.

The square would be bereft of chanting
children, of men at games of chess,
of women bearing home goods from market
and cats who ought be napping on the sills.

My thirteen plots are all the same.
I borrow all my maps.
I fear our journey ends in wind and rain,
cold changeable weather,

the pages torn, the mirror shattered.

Zugswang

She fills jugs of water at the sink
for flowers: mignonette, cotton lavender,
for their scent and fretty form,
sweet pea and love-lies-bleeding,
a token of domestic tragedy, a wound.

He looks up from the chessboard where
he's replaying a famous game of Capablanca's.
He catches her off guard, murmuring
to herself, framed by the door, the blooms.
She wears a dress for a change,
of a sea blue that ebbs to green
when sun floods the kitchen.
Beyond is the window. The sky is an ocean
where clouds like spacecraft or Cuban cigars
float towards the mountain.
He imagines Dutch paintings, bourgeois
interiors, *Woman Washing, Woman Setting
a Table, Woman Bending over a Child*
and conjures a painting half made —
Woman Surrounded by Flowers at a Sink,
himself at an easel mixing pigment and oil,
a north facing studio above a canal
where barges are waiting their turn at the lock
and on the Zuyder Zee scuppy waves rock sailboats.
The landscape surrenders to a polar light.

She arranges the flowers in two jugs.
Lately she has heard her dead mother's voice
tumbling in the drier with the wash:
I told you so, I told you so, I told you so.
The women on the TV in their business suits
and white teeth transmit coded messages,

escape maps buried in their speeches,
though they appear to be reading the news
lest others are watching. Soldiers
have set up a barricade down the road;
they are part of a nationwide search
for a desperate man and his hostage.

A jug in each hand, she moves to the table
and he fancies she has stepped straight into
a Cretan mosaic, a priestess in a Minoan rite,
devotee of the bull, and himself a mosaic worker
fingering a thousand fragments until he finds
the exact shade of blue with that green undertow
to fit his pattern. For her face
and breasts he would use tiles of pure gold;
the alchemists hold it has the exact
calibration of human skin. He will not dwell

on last week's events when he woke
in the night and she was gone. He found her
digging in the garden, her nightgown
drenched through, muck smeared on her arms,
on her legs, the rain lashing down.
She explained that she wanted to be close
to her loved ones, her lost ones,
that they are so cold and lonely in the earth
and they long for the warmth of the living.

She places the flowers on the table.
Any day now she will let go her grip,
surrender herself to the ecstatic freefall.
We are all aware that when she hits bottom
she will shatter into smithereens.
Each shard will reflect the room, the flowers,
the chessboard, and her beloved sky beyond
like a calm ocean lapping at the mountain.

Buying Winkles

My mother would spare me sixpence and say,
'Hurry up now and don't be talking to strange
men on the way.' I'd dash from the ghosts
on the stairs where the bulb had blown
out into Gardiner Street, all relief.
A bonus if the moon was in the strip of sky
between the tall houses, or stars out,
but even in rain I was happy — the winkles
would be wet and glisten blue like little
night skies themselves. I'd hold the tanner tight
and jump every crack in the pavement,
I'd wave up to women at sills or those
lingering in doorways and weave a glad path through
men heading out for the night.

She'd be sitting outside the Rosebowl Bar
on an orange-crate, a pram loaded
with pails of winkles before her.
When the bar doors swung open they'd leak
the smell of men together with drink
and I saw light in golden mirrors.
I envied each soul in the hot interior.

I'd ask her again to show me the right way
to do *it*. She'd take a pin from her shawl —
'Open the eyelid. So. Stick it in
till you feel a grip, then slither him out.
Gently, mind.' The sweetest extra winkle
that brought the sea to me.
'Tell yer Ma I picked them fresh this morning.'

I'd bear the newspaper twists
bulging fat with winkles
proudly home, like torches.

The Pattern

Little has come down to me of hers,
a sewing machine, a wedding band,
a clutch of photos, the sting of her hand
across my face in one of our wars

when we had grown bitter and apart.
Some say that's the fate of the eldest daughter.
I wish now she'd lasted till after
I'd grown up. We might have made a new start

as women without tags like *mother, wife,*
sister, daughter, taken our chances from there.
At forty-two she headed for god knows where.
I've never gone back to visit her grave.

≈

First she'd scrub the floor with Sunlight soap,
an armreach at a time. When her knees grew sore
she'd break for a cup of tea, then start again
at the door with lavender polish. The smell
would percolate back through the flat to us,
her brood banished to the bedroom.

And as she buffed the wax to a high shine
did she catch her own face coming clear?
Did she net a glimmer of her true self?
Did her mirror tell her what mine tells me?

I have her shrug and go on
knowing history has brought her to her knees.

She'd call us in and let us skate around
in our socks. We'd grow solemn as planets
in an intricate orbit about her.

She's bending over crimson cloth,
the younger kids are long in bed.
Late summer, cold enough for a fire,
she works by fading light
to remake an old dress for me.
It's first day back at school tomorrow.

'Pure lambswool. Plenty of wear in it yet.
You know I wore this when I went out with your Da.
I was supposed to be down in a friend's house,
your Granda caught us at the corner.
He dragged me in by the hair — it was long as yours then —
in front of the whole street.
He called your Da every name under the sun,
cornerboy, lout; I needn't tell you
what he called me. He shoved my whole head
under the kitchen tap, took a scrubbing brush
and carbolic soap and in ice-cold water he scrubbed
every spick of lipstick and mascara off my face.
Christ but he was a right tyrant, your Granda.
It'll be over my dead body that anyone harms a hair of your head.'

She must have stayed up half the night
to finish the dress. I found it airing at the fire,
three new copybooks on the table and a bright
bronze nib, St Christopher strung on a silver wire,

as if I were embarking on a perilous journey
to uncharted realms. I wore that dress
with little grace. To me it spelt poverty,
the stigma of the second hand. I grew enough to pass

it on by Christmas to the next in line. I was sizing
up the world beyond our flat patch by patch
daily after school, and fitting each surprising
city street to city square to diamond. I'd watch

the Liffey for hours pulsing to the sea
and the coming and going of ships,
certain that one day it would carry me
to Zanzibar, Bombay, the land of the Ethiops.

There's a photo of her taken in the Phoenix Park
alone on a bench surrounded by roses
as if she had been born to formal gardens.
She stares out as if unaware
that any human hand held the camera, wrapped
entirely in her own shadow, the world beyond her
already a dream, already lost. She's
eight months pregnant. Her last child.

Her steel needles sparked and clacked,
the only other sound a settling coal
or her sporadic mutter
at a hard part in the pattern.
She favoured sensible shades:
Moss Green, Mustard, Beige.

I dreamt a robe of a colour
so pure it became a word.

Sometimes I'd have to kneel
an hour before her by the fire,
a skein around my outstretched hands,
while she rolled wool into balls.
If I swam like a kite too high
amongst the shadows on the ceiling
or flew like a fish in the pools
of pulsing light, she'd reel me firmly
home, she'd land me at her knees.

Tongues of flame in her dark eyes,
she'd say, 'One of these days I must
teach you to follow a pattern.'

Ard Fheis

Down through the cigarette smoke
the high windows cast
ecstatic light to the floorboards
stiletto pocked and butt scorched

but now such golden pools of sun to bask in there.
I am fish
water my demesne.
The room pulses in, then out, of focus

and all this talk of the people, of who we are,
of what we need, is robbed of meaning,
becomes sub-melody, sonic undertow,
a room of children chanting off

by heart a verse. I'm nine or ten,
the Central Model School,
Miss Shannon beats out the metre
with her stick.

I wind up in the ghost place
the language rocks me to,
a cobwebby state, chilled vault
littered with our totems;

a tattered Starry Plough,
a bloodstained Proclamation,
Connolly strapped wounded to a chair,
May blossom in Kilmainham.

I am following my father's steps
on a rainy Sunday in the National Museum,

by talisman of torc, carved spiral,
síle na gig's yoni made luscious in stone.

And somewhere there is vestige
of my mother nursing me to sleep,
when all my world was touch,
and possibly was peace.

I float down to a September evening,
the Pro-Cathedral, girls in rows at prayer,
gaze at the monstrance, lulled to adoration,
mesmeric in frankincense and candlelight:

Hail our life our sweetness and our hope
to thee do we cry poor banished children of Eve
to thee do we send up our sighs
mourning and weeping in this valley of tears.

I push back to the surface, break clear,
the light has come on fluorescent
and banishes my dreaming self.
It is, after all, an ordinary room

and we are ordinary people.
We pull our collars up and head
for the new moon sky of our city
fondling each whorled bead in our macabre rosary.

Don't even speak to me of Stephen the Martyr,
the host snug in his palm,
slipping through the wounded streets
to keep his secret safe.

Two-Buck Tim From Timbucktoo

I found it in the granary under rubble
where the back gable caved in,
a 78 miraculously whole in a nest of smashed records,
as if it had been hatched by a surreal hen,
a pullet with a taste for the exotic.

I took it in and swabbed it down,
put it on the turntable and filled the cottage
with its scratchy din. Ghosts of the long dead
flocked from their narrow grooves beneath foreign soils
to foxtrot round my kitchen in the dusk.

I'd say Leitrim in the forties was every bit as depressed
as Leitrim is today, the young were heading off
in droves, the same rain fell all winter long.
Eventually one old woman was left looking at her hands
while the Bell Boys of Broadway played 'Two Buck Tim from
    Timbuctoo',

and dreamt her daughters back about the place, the swing of
    a skirt,
a face caught in lamplight, with every revolution of the disc.
This winter I have grown unduly broody. As I go
about my daily work an otherworldly mantra turns
within my head: Two Buck Tim from Timbuctoo,

Two Buck Tim from Timbuctoo. It keeps me up at night.
I roam about the rooms. I hope to catch them at it.
I want to rend the veil, step out onto their plane,
spiral down a rain-washed road, let some ghostly partner
take the lead, become at last another migrant soul.

Elegy for a Child

It is not that the spring brings
you back. Birds riotous about
the house, fledglings learn to fly.

Nor that coming on petals drifted in the orchard
is like opening your door, a draught of pastel,
a magpie hoard of useless bright.

Clouds move over the river
under the sun — a cotton sheet shook out.
The pines bring me news
from deeper in the woods:
the rain will come sing on the roof soon.

It is not the day's work in the garden,
the seedlings neatly leafmould mulched in lines.
Not the woodpile trim bespeaking good husbandry,
conjuring up the might-have-been.

It is not the anarchic stream
in a stone-sucking dash past the crane's haunt, fickle,
sky mirror now, now shattered bauble,

nor the knowledge of planets in proper order,
their passage through my fourth house
fixed before I was born.
It is not that the night you died
a star plummeted to earth.
It is not that I watched it fall.

It is not that I was your mother,
nor the rooted deep down loss,

that has brought me this moment
to sit by the window and weep.

You were but a small bird balanced
within me
ready for flight.

Child Burial

I chose your grave clothes with care,
your favourite stripey shirt,

your blue cotton trousers.
They smelt of woodsmoke, of October,

your own smell there too.
I chose a gansy of handspun wool,

warm and fleecy for you. It is
so cold down in the dark.

No light can reach you and teach you
the paths of wild birds,

the names of the flowers,
the fishes, the creatures.

Ignorant you must remain
of the sun and its work,

my lamb, my calf, my eaglet,
my cub, my kid, my nestling,

my suckling, my colt. I would spin
time back, take you again

within my womb, your amniotic lair,
and further spin you back

through nine waxing months
to the split seeding moment

you chose to be made flesh,
word within me.

I'd cancel the love feast
the hot night of your making.

I would travel alone
to a quiet mossy place,

you would spill from me into the earth
drop by bright red drop.

No Go Area

In the first zone
you will be stripped and searched
for hidden weapons.

In the second zone
you must know their language
or they'll finger you as other.

In the third zone
bribe the guard — it's quicker.
The beast is quite tame by day.

In the fourth zone
an oxygen mask is mandatory.
There they stack the bodies.

In the fifth zone
it is all sex and experiments.
Few ever go this far.

In the sixth zone
you might have trouble in the dark
knowing if you are beast or offering.

In the seventh zone
stands the gate to the no go area.
Go, God help you, there you're on your own.

Her Heroin Dream

She dreamt the moon a gaudy egg,
a Chinese gimcrack. When it hatched,
a young dragon would spiral to earth
trailing garnet and emerald sparks,
shrieking through the ozone layer,
the citizens blinded by dragon-glory.

In the heart of night would blaze a light
greater than the sun, supernova fierce.

The Liffey and the two canals would vanish
and Dublin bay evaporate, leaving beached
spiny prawns and crabs, coiled sea snails,
a dead sailor's shoe, shipping wrecks,
radioactive waste in Saharas of sand.
The buildings would scorch to black stumps,
windows melt, railroads buckle,
bricks fallen to dust would sift
in dervish swirls along the thoroughfares.

Each tree in the town would turn torch
to celebrate his passing.

She would wait in her cell.
He'd enter softly in the guise of a youth:
his eyes the blue of hyacinth,
his skin like valerian,
his lips Parthian red.
He'd take her from behind.
The kundalini energy would shoot straight up her spine,
blow her head open like a flower.
Dragon seed would root deep in her womb.
Dragon nature course through her veins.

They'd slip from the cell hands twined,
glide over the prison wall into a new morning
to sport among the ruins.

The Man who Lives in the Clouds

You said if we reached the top
we'd find the navel of the earth,
proof that matter was a mere prop,
a gift, our right from birth,

to keep us occupied through time,
that energy alone was real.
I was breathless from the climb.
I wanted a bed and a decent meal.

I was sick of the dirt, the reek of yak
butter seeping from my haversack,
the prospect of another night,
the endless talk of humanity's plight,

of philosophers' stones and holy grails.
I wanted nothing more than to stand
humbly on the lower slopes and gaze
at the peaks, and whether I was damned

or saved was much of a muchness to me.
You claimed the dead lived deep inside
the mountain, that they clamoured to be free.
I heard only the wind lash like a tide

race through the trees. I left
you then and made for home, deaf
to your threats, your curses. Now
I lead a quiet life in the village below.

I've a clutch of hens, a herb patch, a video
and a black cat. I do not think of you
up there with your yetis, your eagles, your thunderbolts,
and your dense cloud cover the sun can't break through.

The Dark Twin

for Seanie Lambe

You believe
they contract when you turn to the window —
there's a girl in pink passing
you might or might not know
down a street you say history will be made on
as the woman you hold turns to your eyes.
Anemones, she tells you, make the same sound as pupils.
Pishew, pishew, were you close enough
in rockpool silence, is what you would hear.

And you believe
she'll turn again and again to your eyes
as you hold her. Show your stored wisdom
in a ritual of healing. Your hands move
over her dark form. She can't refuse you.
Gulls cross the sky, bells sound for first Mass.
You know she'll seek you for she is
your dark twin. Her eyes don't reflect you.
Her pupils are still as the dark pool
she grew from. She names you *diablo*.
If you enter her now you can teach her
the nature of history, the city that's made her.
She'll name a price later and say you've had
her cheaply. She'll be just. You won't haggle
but find the exact change and count it into her palm.

And you believe
she'll return and desire you once more —
more than her own life, more than her darkness.
This you know surely as you glance over

her eyes to the girl in pink passing.
You move above her: by your ritual rocking
you'll move her to tears.
She'll learn to accept love though still
you must pay her the exact amount due.

And you believe
you can quieten her sobs in the morning
when she tells you again
how the world will succumb to men in dark uniforms.
You believe she has stood, her face to a stone wall,
while the men cock their rifles and wait for the order.
You know she's been there. You know you can heal her.
The burns from the bombings will ease as you rock her.
The legs that are mangled made whole for fast dancing.
Her sobs will be songs for the rearing of children.
Still you must pay her the exact amount due.

And you believe all this
as you turn from the window,
the girl in pink passing at the moment
you enter your dark twin. Your pupils
dilate, your breath as it leaves you
makes the one word you can never repay her.

Lullaby

for Brenda Meehan

My sister is sleeping
and makes small murmurs
as she turns in a dream

she is swinging a child
under the shade of
a lilac tree blooming

in a garden in springtime
my sister is sleeping.

The rain falls
on Finglas
to each black roof

it lashes a story
of time on the ocean
of moon on the river

and flashes down drainpipes
into deep gutters.

My sister is sleeping
her hands full of blossoms
plucked for the child

who dreams in her womb
rocked in tall branches
close to the stars

where my sister is sleeping
within her small child.

The Statue of the Virgin at Granard Speaks

It can be bitter here at times like this,
November wind sweeping across the border.
Its seeds of ice would cut you to the quick.
The whole town tucked up safe and dreaming,
even wild things gone to earth, and I
stuck up here in this grotto, without as much as
star or planet to ease my vigil.

The howling won't let up. Trees
cavort in agony as if they would be free
and take off — ghost voyagers
on the wind that carries intimations
of garrison towns, walled cities, ghetto lanes
where men hunt each other and invoke
the various names of God as blessing
on their death tactics, their night manoeuvres.
Closer to home the wind sails over
dying lakes. I hear fish drowning.
I taste the stagnant water mingled
with turf smoke from outlying farms.

They call me Mary — Blessed, Holy, Virgin.
They fit me to a myth of a man crucified:
the scourging and the falling, and the falling again,
the thorny crown, the hammer blow of iron
into wrist and ankle, the sacred bleeding heart.
They name me Mother of all this grief
though mated to no mortal man.
They kneel before me and their prayers
fly up like sparks from a bonfire
that blaze a moment, then wink out.

It can be lovely here at times. Springtime,
early summer. Girls in Communion frocks
pale rivals to the riot in the hedgerows
of cow parsley and haw blossom, the perfume
from every rushy acre that's left for hay
when the light swings longer with the sun's push north.

Or the grace of a midsummer wedding
when the earth herself calls out for coupling
and I would break loose of my stony robes,
pure blue, pure white, as if they had robbed
a child's sky for their colour. My being
cries out to be incarnate, incarnate,
maculate and tousled in a honeyed bed.

Even an autumn burial can work its own pageantry.
The hedges heavy with the burden of fruiting
crab, sloe, berry, hip; clouds scud east
pear scented, windfalls secret in long
orchard grasses, and some old soul is lowered
to his kin. Death is just another harvest
scripted to the season's play.

But on this All Souls' Night there is
no respite from the keening of the wind.
I would not be amazed if every corpse came risen
from the graveyard to join in exaltation with the gale,
a cacophony of bone imploring sky for judgement
and release from being the conscience of the town.

On a night like this I remember the child
who came with fifteen summers to her name,
and she lay down alone at my feet
without midwife or doctor or friend to hold her hand
and she pushed her secret out into the night,

far from the town tucked up in little scandals,
bargains struck, words broken, prayers, promises,
and though she cried out to me *in extremis*
I did not move,
I didn't lift a finger to help her,
I didn't intercede with heaven,
nor whisper the charmed word in God's ear.

On a night like this I number the days to the solstice
and the turn back to the light.
                       O sun,
centre of our foolish dance,
burning heart of stone,
molten mother of us all,
hear me and have pity.

Fruit

Alone in the room
with the statue of Venus
I couldn't resist
cupping her breast.

It was cool
and heavy in my hand
like an apple.

Night Walk: Effernagh to Eslin

Earth shadows the moon,
leaves just a paring
of light to get home by.

You follow iced potholes
that gleam in the dark,
pebbles, perhaps, dropped by a child

when her father and mother
have left her to find her
own way out of the forest.

A stream weeps. The lake
past blackthorn hedges
is waiting for *finder*

to keep her. And you
still have three miles to go,
three miles to go and

no promise of sleep, but
the long night vigil
and drowning in pools

that go down forever
and there's no way out
and the bottom is never.

Mist grazes a meadow,
spills through a gap
to fresh pasture.

You have to get home.
Someone is waiting
The table is set.

The kettle near boiling,
the clock ticks louder.
He paces the floor

from chair to window,
sees nothing outside
but himself looking in.

At the top of the hill
you make out a light
between pine and willow.

The last mile it measures
your step on the road,
human in the darkness.

Home by Starlight

for Lisa Steppe

You ask me which I prefer —
the stars themselves or their mirror
image on the puddles of our path
home. Their light as strong
as moonlight, the night cold and still.
We take a shortcut across an overgrown rath,
old stones that seem to spill
haphazardly, but if you haul back the long
ivy tendrils, hack through the brambles, you
will find patterns there, you

will know lifetimes ago we gazed
at the same constellations amazed
by such brilliance, and found in their rule
the measure of each year, each journey.
Do you remember how it was?
The seasons of study in the star school
scanning for portent conjugations
of sky beasts which peopled the sea
of our heavens. Do you remember
that crazy light we tracked one mid-winter?

The light they later called the Christos,
and the terror, the blood cost of that Logos?
How our arts were eclipsed and many
gentle comrades tortured and burned?
How the songs we had crafted for travel
were lost, language itself lost,
when we were scattered like sparks to the wind? So well
you might ask — the light, or its image, turned

in a puddle, surefooted friend on the path you roam
by the light of a million million suns home.

You Open Your Hands to Me

They hold nothing
They are calloused
Earth under the fingernails
The heart line strong and sure
As any river crazy for the sea

These hands hold nothing
They are the hands of a worker
They are the hands of one who has no job

They have tucked a whole city up at night
And in the morning cast it adrift

These hands could pack everything they value
In a minute or less

From a burning building
They would save what is living
Not what is Art

They reach to me in the dark
Of a nightmare
They pull me clear
They place the particular stars I prefer
At my window
On cloudy nights
They make images of the moon
In case I am lonely

These hands hold nothing
They do not judge
They are drawn to the wounded

They have no history
They fire the first shot

They are the hands of a builder
They dismantle empires
They love most what is wild
They invite no pity

Were I dying I would choose
These hands to guide me
Out of the world

You open your hands to me
Your empty hands

Coda

You open the hated book,
it is the book of my self.
The more that you read there
the fainter the print becomes
until the letters are faded,
white nests protected by the page.

I gave up on the window box:
leaves went transparent,
eaten away by greenfly.
When you come home you'll find
geranium ghosts, spectral nasturtiums,
a flock of albino butterflies
settled on the sill. I'll be hung

up in the larder by the heels,
dressed as a deer would be,
my skin in a casual heap on the floor.
You can wear it if you wish
though flesh clings to parts,
especially the extremities. Still,
a sharp flint stone could do the trick.

It should be a comfortable fit.
There's a note in the dresser
on French seams and buttonholes
lest you need to alter any part.
The breasts will be a problem;
you'll need the smallest crewel for the job
and the good new scissors of German steel.
The offcuts may be useful somewhere else.

Put the rest of me on at gas mark 3,
(you know those stringy muscles in my back!).
Don't forget to baste me now and then.
Don't bring your current lover home to tea,
there's just enough for one. Besides
I'm an acquired taste, like squid
or pickled limes. I wouldn't delay —
were I you I'd catch the earliest ferry
else the worms will have their way with me.

You'd come upon me bleached and empty
in the cool larder rafters, the slates blown down,
green garden light nesting in my bones.

The Man who was Marked by Winter

He was heading for Bridal Veil Falls,
an upward slog on a dusty path.
Mid May and hot as a mill-

stone grinding his shoulders, his back.
Each breath was a drowning.
And who's to say if it was a mirage

the other side of the creek's brown
water. He saw it, that's enough,
in the deep shade of a rocky overhang —

the spoor of winter, a tracery of ice. If
we'd reached him, we'd have warned him of the depth,
the secret current underneath.

He must have been half crazy with the heat.
He stripped off. Waded in.
His feet were cut from under him. He was swept

downriver in melt water from the mountain.
She clutched him to her breast, that beast of winter.
One look from her agate eyes and he abandoned

hope. He was pliant. She pulled him under.
If she had him once, she had him thrice.
She shook his heart and mind asunder.

And he would willingly have gone back to her palace
or her lair, whichever; whatever she was,
he would have lived forever in her realms of ice.

She must have grown tired of his human ways.
We found him tossed like a scrap on the bank,
hours or years or seconds later. His eyes

stared straight at the sun. His past is a blank
snowfield where no one will step. She made her mark
below his heart, a five-fingered gash — *Bondsman.*

Insomnia

Pale under the moon
through the glass
his limbs still
and soon
before stormclouds pass
over the house and fill

it with darkness she'll slip
in beside him
as into a pool.
Warm ripples will lap
her thighs, brim
her breasts, spool

her close and free
her mind of the trouble
that has kept her late
by the fire, a fragrancy
of applewood, to struggle
with her fate

which has always been
to leave what is familiar,
trusted, known,
for the half-seen
shadow world, far
beyond the human zone.

Three Paintings of York Street

for Ita Kelly

BEFORE THE PUBS CLOSE

Quick. Before the moon is eaten
by that cloud, rescue its dust,
sift it over the shopping centre,
the student hostel, that couple
hand in hand walking to the Green.
And quick. Before last orders and drunken cries
steal the breath the street is holding,
exhale it lovingly below each window
to reclaim from night the shadowy areas.

Salt your canvas with a woman
quietly weeping in a tenement room
until her tears become a blessing
sprinkled from your fingers,
those spatters of intense blue
beside the three black cats
who wait with ... patience, is it?
on a granite step for you to find
the exact amber of their eyes
as they gaze at the moon.

WOMAN FOUND DEAD BEHIND SALVATION ARMY HOSTEL

You will have to go outside for this one.
The night is bitter cold
but you must go out,
you could not invent this.

You can make a quick sketch
and later, in your studio, mix the colours,
the purple, the eerie green of her bruises,
the garish crimson of her broken mouth.

For consolation there's the line
her spine makes as it remembers
its beginnings, as if at the very end
she turned foetal and knew again
the roar of her mother's blood in her ears,
the drum of her mother's heart
before she drowned in the seventh wave
beyond pain, or your pity.

Your hand will steady as you draw the cobbles.
They impose a discipline, the comfort of habit,
as does the symmetry of brick walls
which define the alley and whose very height
cut off the light and hid
the beast who maimed her.

CHILDREN OF YORK STREET AT PLAY IN THE COLLEGE OF SURGEONS' CARPARK

You worry given the subject
about sentimentality, about indulgence,
but as you work
the children turn to pattern
and you may as well be
weaving in a Turkish bazaar, one eye
on your son lest he topple to the tarmac.
And your fingers of their own volition
find the perfect stress between warp and weft.
Your mind can lope as loosely
as a gazelle through savannah
or nimble as a mountain goat,
attain an unexpected purchase on a sheer
cliff face, or you may be dolphin
and cavort the prismatic ranges
of the green sea's depth.
                                        And after,
cleaning brushes, you will wonder
why no child can be discerned
on your canvas, why there is no bike,
no skateboard, no skipping rope,
no carpark, why your colours are
all primary, pure as you can make them,
why in your pattern the shapes keep shifting
like flighty spirits threatening
to burst into song.

My Love about his Business in the Barn

You're fiddling with something in the barn,
a makeshift yoke for beans to climb,
held together like much in our lives
with blue baling twine, scraps of chicken wire.

Such a useless handyman: our world could collapse,
frequently *has* with a huff and a puff.
You'd hoke a length of string from your back pocket,
humming a Woody Guthrie song, you'd bind

the lintel to stone, the slate to rafter,
'It'll do for the minute if the wind stays down.'
And so I've learned to live with dodgy matter:
shelves that tumble to the floor if you glance

at them sideways; walls that were not built
for leaning against; a great chasm in the kitchen
crossable only by a rope bridge; a blow hole
by our bed where the Atlantic spouts.

On stormy nights it drenches the walls, the ceiling.
Days you come home reeking of Brut and brimstone
I suspect you've been philandering underground
and not breaking your back beyond on the bog.

So is it any wonder when I see you
mooching in the barn this fine May morning,
a charm of finches lending local colour,
that I rush for my holy water, my rabbit's foot?

That I shut my eyes tight and wait
for the explosion, then the silence,
then the sweet aftershock when the earth
skids under me, when stars and deep space usurp my day?

Mysteries of the Home

The soul stands lonely in its choice,
Waiting, itself a slow thing,
In the changing body.
— Theodore Roethke

WELL

I know this path by magic not by sight.
Behind me on the hillside the cottage light
is like a star that's gone astray. The moon
is waning fast, each blade of grass a rune
inscribed by hoarfrost. This path's well worn.
I lug a bucket by bramble and blossoming blackthorn.
I know this path by magic not by sight.
Next morning when I come home quite unkempt
I cannot tell what happened at the well.
You spurn my explanation of a sex spell
cast by the spirit that guards the source
that boils deep in the belly of the earth,
even when I show you what lies strewn
in my bucket — a golden waning moon,
seven silver stars, our own porch light,
your face at the window staring into the dark.

QUEEN

Go then. Don't let me stand in your way.
I hope you'll be very happy. She's quite
pretty if you like that type. Not a hair astray,
all that jangly jewellery, teeth so white
and even. Are they real? She's like a queen,
you a subject yoked to plod her wake.
I who spurn vanity admit
a fascination with her nails, long, sharp,
red as rosehips flashing in autumn dusk.
That dress — lotus flowers on a field of green,
just the thing to swan around your bedsit
in. Forgive me if I harp.
I never meant to nag you, act the wife,
it's just your cringing wounds me like a knife.

HERMIT

I'll go out into the world now.
If I meet a snake I'll charm it.
It'll wind round my staff and grow
timid as a lamb. I'll keep
some books and work by night for choice.
You can have the daily kingdom,
you can have the pots, the pans, the sheets.
you can have the home, the garden.
My body will be my shelter. I'll
keel off like a snail. If
on a moonlit night you see my glistening tracks
and are overcome by remorse — tough.
I'll survive on air and scholarship
and the delight of my own voice
making songs and prayers
and, if I'm greatly blessed, a poem or two.

KING

When I came to your inner chamber
having fought through the ranks of shadowy petitioners
you gave me the glad eye and sent
a note by a trusted courtier.
You promised a life of ease,
a place to work in peace,
songbirds and panthers, never
a worry about where the next meal was coming from,
no more hiding from the rent man, the ESB man,
the wolfman gnawing at my door.
And when you had me, burned me out,
you placed my ashes in your collection.
Number 8. A fine woman.
Pity about her accent though.

SEED

The first warm day of spring
and I step out in the garden from the gloom
of a house where hope had died
to tally the storm damage, to seek what may
have survived. And finding some forgotten
lupins I'd sown from seed last autumn
holding in their fingers a raindrop each
like a peace offering, or a promise,
I am suddenly grateful and would
offer a prayer if I believed in god.
But not believing, I bless the power of seed,
its casual, useful persistence,
and bless the power of sun,
its conspiracy with the underground
and thank my stars the winter's ended.

from

Pillow Talk

(1994)

for Nora Harkin

My Father Perceived as a Vision of St. Francis

for Brendan Kennelly

It was the piebald horse in next door's garden
frightened me out of a dream
with her dawn whinny. I was back
in the boxroom of the house,
my brother's room now,
full of ties and sweaters and secrets.
Bottles chinked on the doorstep,
the first bus pulled up to the stop.
The rest of the house slept

except for my father. I heard
him rake the ash from the grate,
plug in the kettle, hum a snatch of a tune.
Then he unlocked the back door
and stepped out into the garden.

Autumn was nearly done, the first frost
whitened the slates of the estate.
He was older than I had reckoned,
his hair completely silver,
and for the first time I saw the stoop
of his shoulder, saw that
his leg was stiff. What's he at?
So early and still stars in the west?

They came then: birds
of every size, shape, colour; they came
from the hedges and shrubs,
from eaves and garden sheds,
from the industrial estate, outlying fields,

71

from Dubber Cross they came
and the ditches of the North Road.

The garden was a pandemonium
when my father threw up his hands
and tossed the crumbs to the air. The sun

cleared O'Reilly's chimney
and he was suddenly radiant,
a perfect vision of St. Francis,
made whole, made young again,
in a Finglas garden.

A Child's Map of Dublin

I wanted to find you Connolly's Starry Plough,
the flag I have lived under since birth or since
I first scanned nightskies and learned the nature of work.
'That hasn't been on show in years,' the porter told us.
They're revising at the National Museum,
all hammers and drills and dust, converting to
an interpretive centre in the usual contemporary style.

The Natural History Museum: found poem
of oriole, kingfisher, sparrowhawk, nightjar,
but the gull drew me strongest — childhood guide
to the freedom and ecstasy of flight. Common
cacophonist, nothing romantic about that squabbler
of windowledges, invader of the one p.m. schoolyard,
wakefollower of sailors. But watch him on a clear ocean

and nothing reads the wind so well. In the updraught
of a sudden love, I walk the northside streets
that whelped me; not a brick remains
of the tenement I reached the age of reason in. Whole
streets are remade, the cranes erect over Eurocrat schemes
down the docks. There is nothing
to show you there, not a trace of a girl

in ankle socks and hand-me-downs, sulking
on a granite step when she can't raise the price of a film,
or a bus to the beach. The movie she ran in her head?
Africa — hostage slave to some Berber prince or, chainmailed,
she is heroine of a hopeless war
spurring her men to death, but honourable death.

Better I take you up Cumberland Street Saturday.
We'll hoke out something foreign and erotic,
from the mounds of cast-offs on the path.
And when the market's over we'll wander home,
only go the streets that are our fancy.
You'll ask me no questions. I'll tell you no lies.

Climb in here between the sheets
in the last light of this April evening. We'll trust
the charts of our bodies. They've brought us
safe to each other, battle-scarred and frayed
at the folds, they'll guide us to many wonders.
Come, let's play in the backstreets and tidal flats
till we fall off the edge of the known world,

and drown.

The Other Woman

That night when you entered her for the first time
she was the lonely city, and you were a man with a key
to a room in a house on a street where you might go out of
    the rain
and sit by the window to drink lemon vodka

with no tales to tell, no questions, no answers, no
hope of tomorrow. Not silence; but breath and the fall
of rain to the garden. No light but streetlight.
She was in shadow. You were a stranger and all

she could trust was what she read of your path
when you held out your hand and said come.
She was scribed on your fateline, her own name there
was a song half-remembered, hot on your tongue,

hot on the white sheets you tangled your selves up in.
They were your sails and she was the port in every girl
you knew you were born free for; and bound
to the rule of the sea, her grief, her pulse, her moody

river, her sulky moons, the way they hid for months
under cloud, you were humble. I understood all this
when she woke the next morning to rain on the city.
For my work I need starlight preferably

and plenty of time on my hands. I made her dream
sunshine, a tower, a golden fish atop it, a street
running down to a harbour, a ship just docked,
a stranger approaching with the key to her door.

City

HEARTH

What is the fire you draw to
when you clutch each other
between the sheets? What cold do
you fear? What drives you near
madness, the jealousy you daily
bear? That tyrant time
sifting through the glass. Tell me
a story, not in rhyme
or made up fancy but plain
as the ash in the grate.
The window pane rattles, the rain
beats about the house. Late
drinkers are turfed from the bar. Wind
snatches their song, tosses it down-
river to the sea pulsing in your mind.
You slip your moorings, cruise the town.

NIGHT WALK

Out here you can breathe.
Between showers, the street
empty. Forget your lover
faithless in the chilly bed
who'll wake soon and wonder
if you've left for good.
Granite under your feet
glitters, nearby a siren. Threat

or a promise? You take Fumbally Lane
to the Blackpitts, cut back by the canal.
Hardly a sound you've made, creature
of night in grey jeans and desert boots,
familiar of shade. Listen.
                              The train
bearing chemicals to Mayo, a dog far off, the fall
of petals to the paths of the Square,
a child screaming in a third floor flat.

On Mount Street high heels clack,
stumble in their rhythm, resume.
Let her too get home safe, your prayer,
not like that poor woman last night
dragged down Glovers Alley, raped there,
battered to a pulp. Still unnamed.
Your key in the door, you've made it back,
a chorus of birds predicting light.

MAN SLEEPING

How deep are you, how far under?
Here's rosemary I stole on my walk
and the first lilac from the Square.
I lay them on the quilt. You talk
in your dreaming. *I am the beating tide,*
mine is the shore. Taste of the sea,
pulse of my heart. *Don't leave me,*
don't leave me. I dive beneath
and you stiffen to my mouth.
You'll be deep within me when you wake,
your pulse my own. Wave that I ride,
I'll take everything before you break.

FULL MOON

She's up there. You'd know the pull,
stretching you tight as a drumhead,
anywhere. This morning lull
between the alarm and quitting the bed
you consider the scrawb on his back —
sigil of grief: the thumbscrew, the rack.
A paleskin staked on the desert floor
bound at ankle, at neck, at wrist,
no cavalry in sight to even the score.
This is the knife in the gut; this is its twist.

She's up there. Tonight they'll dish out
more downers in prison, in the mental
asylum, tonight there'll be more blood spilt
on the street, and you will howl
to her through the tattered cloud scrawled
across the windowpane, a howl fated
by the blemish on his shoulderblade.
Ask yourself: *To what shapechanger has he mated?*

ON THE WARPATH

The full moon is drawing you tight
as a drumhead. Your face in the mirror
is cloudy, overcast. No sunny spells;
frost inland tonight.

Reconnoitre the terrain of the heart,
scan for high ground. Ambush, skirmish,
reprisal, this deadly game you play.
Give as good as you get.

Choose protective colouring, camouflage,
know your foe, every move of him,
every bar of his battle hymn.
Though the outward face is dead cas-

ual, within the self is coiled
unsprung, the human, suddenly, wild.

Not Your Muse

I'm not your muse, not that creature
in the painting, with the beautiful body,
Venus on the half-shell. Can
you not see I'm an ordinary woman
tied to the moon's phases, bloody
six days in twenty-eight? Sure
I'd like to leave you in love's blindness,
cherish the comfort of your art, the way
it makes me whole and shining,
smooths the kinks of my habitual distress,
never mentions how I stumble into the day,
fucked up, penniless, on the verge of whining

at my lot. You'd have got away with it once.
In my twenties I often traded a bit
of sex for immortality. That's a joke.
Another line I swallowed, hook
and sinker. Look at you —
rapt, besotted. Not a gesture that's true

on that canvas, not a droopy breast,
wrinkle or stretchmark in sight.
But if it keeps you happy who am I
to charge in battledressed to force you test
your painted doll against the harsh light
I live by, against a brutal merciless sky.

Good Friday, 1991

The low tide reveals him
tangled in plastic and branches
snagged at the foot of Capel Street bridge.

How he came to be there,
whether he jumped off
the quay wall or slipped
quietly into the green water,
another city mystery.
                                    And what
of the children watching?
The fire brigade, the grappling hooks,
the boat inching up the shallows;
what of the soul manhandling
the body over the stern
who looks up suddenly to our staring faces?

Though we glimpsed his face
but briefly, it's there before me now
white as the snow of Komarovo,
his slender drenched body
that no arms can succour,
his song and pattern ended
under the fast spring clouds,
a strong wind from the east
ruffling the low Liffey waters.

Laburnum

You walk into an ordinary room
an ordinary evening, say
mid May, when the laburnum

hangs over the railings of the Square
and the city is lulled by eight o'clock,
the traffic sparse, the air fresher.

You expect to find someone
waiting though now you live
alone. You've answered none

of your calls. The letters pile
up in the corner. The idea
persists that someone waits while

you turn the brass handle and knock
on the light. Gradually
the dark seeps into the room. You lock

out the night, scan a few books.
It's days since you ate.
The plants are dying — even the cactus,

shrivelled like an old scrotum
has given up the ghost. There's
a heel of wine in a magnum

you bought, when? The day
before? The day before that?
It's the only way

out. The cold sweats
begin. You knock back a few.
You've no clean clothes left.

He is gone. Say it.
Say it to yourself, to the room.
Say it loud enough to believe it.

You will live breath
by breath. The beat of your own heart
will scourge you. You'll wait

in vain, for he's gone from you.
And every night is a long
slide to the dawn you

wake to, terrified in your ordinary room
on an ordinary morning, say
mid May, say the time of laburnum.

Playing House

You have prepared a room for me,
a desk below a high window
giving on coachhouses, lanes,
a wild garden of elder and ash.

Home, you say, let this be
a home for you. Unpack
your clothes, hang them
beside mine. Put your sharp
knife in my kitchen, your books
in my stacks. Let your face
share my mirrors. Light
fires in my hearth. Your talismans
are welcome. Break bread
with me. Settle. Settle.

'When you left the city you carried ...'

When you left the city you carried
off the May sun, left heavy skies.
A bad spell was cast on the island:
colour leached from blossom, birds fell mute,
the Liffey stopped dreaming of the sea,
the eyes of the citizenry grew frosty
and for two weeks now I have moved
like a zombie through my life.
All I turn my hand to
snags. I can't sleep nights. I fret,
demented with desire for your body
weaving in sea motion under mine.
Close to dawn I hit the streets
and walk in hope of losing you,
in hope of peace. Christ I'd give
ten years of my span to look on your face
for an instant, to fall into your eyes
that are the sea blue of desert mornings,
to dive through the fiery coronas,
drown in the depths of your pupils.
Days are spent in superstitious rite:
penny candles at Valentine's shrine,
invocations to an Eastern goddess
to please watch over your journey,
to bring you home safe,
and if anyone should lay a finger on you
or harm a hair of your head
there'll be no hiding from my wrath
on this, or any other, planet.

Pillow Talk

These hot midsummer nights I whisper
assignations, trysts, heather beds
I'd like to lay you down in, remote beaches
we could escape to, watch
bonfire sparks mix with stars.
I want you to stay alive till we two
meet again, to hold the line, to ignore
the gossip traded about me in the marketplace.
I fall back on cliché, the small
change of an adulterous summer,
plots of half-hatched movies, theories
of forked lightning, how you make
the soles of my feet burn when I come.

What you don't hear is the other voice
when she speaks through me
beyond human pity or mercy. She wants you.
Put her eye on you the first time
she saw you. And I'm powerless,
a slave to her whim. She shall
have you. What can I do
when she speaks of white river stones,
elfin grots, her sacred birds?
I know she once tore a man apart,
limb from limb with her bare hands
in some rite in her bloody past.
My stomach turns at the hot
relentless stench of her history.

Nights you stare out
panic-stricken through the mask,
I think you may have heard her speak:

you realise that you ride a demon,
that the dark has no end to it.
Though I mean you no grief,
I cannot vouchsafe her intent. I fear
not all my healing arts can salve
the wound she has in store for you.

Silk

You dance in a length of shiny silk
lately acquired in a Tashkent bazaar,
charming me with every slink
of your hips, teeth aflash.

Haven't we met somewhere
before — by a gypsy fire
or in a blue domed marketplace
where slaves are traded for new gold?

If you seek to bind me
this summer with sex and cool melon,
don't bother. I'm already bound
and lost and falling fast,

tumbling head over heels
down the abyss.
                    To think
I've waited centuries for this!
You dancing in shiny silk

in the afternoon, stealing an hour
from work. And where
does it end?
                    Work and love:
the heart's hunger, the daily bread.

Breagaim Breagaim Breagaim
I woo I lie I woo
and if you walk away from me
on a hot city street

I'll not look after you,

                                      but turn
into my own mystery. Though
it may take centuries to find you again,
dancing wantonly in silk.

Aubade

after an image by Joan Miró

And then we dress for the June sun.
You hand me a small bird to guard me,
to make a song only I can hear.
We part on the corner; I spin
like a top through the city,
through the hot streets.
Nothing can harm me.
Nothing disturb me.
Not all the tantric fruit on Moore Street
the beggar's cupped hand,
the grey suited ones,
the kept ladies of the rich,
the men with rape in their hearts,
the dole queue blues,
the priest sweating in black,
the sleazy deals of our rulers,
the prisoner in her pox hole of a cell,
the warder and her grating keys,
the enbalmer's curious art,
the thunderbolts of a Catholic god,
the useless tears of his mother.
You've given me a small bird
to guard me, to sing me spinning songs,
the gift of our journey
and a safe place to rest in.
I stand in that centre,
the still place you grant me,
just like any other woman
with a bird in front of the sun.

Would you jump into my grave as quick?

Would you jump into my grave as quick?
my granny would ask when one of us took
her chair by the fire. You, woman,
done up to the nines, red lips a come on,
your breath reeking of drink
and your black eye on my man tonight
in a Dublin bar, think
first of the steep drop, the six dark feet.

The Ghost of My Mother Comforts Me

after Van Morrison

Do not fear, daughter,
when they lift their sticks, their stones,
when they hiss beneath their breaths —

Fallen woman, adulteress, breaker of marriage vows
made before a holy priest to an honourable man.

For you, daughter, there is no blame,
for you no portion of guilt,
for you're made in my likeness.
You can take the crucifixion from your voice.
I will stroke your forehead till you sleep,
till you pass over into the dreamworld
where we can walk together in gardens wet with rain
or fly along old star roads
or sit quietly near running water.

And when you wake refreshed
you'll be ready for their sticks, their stones,
their names that cannot hurt you.
Balance your gypsy soul, lodged
in the body given you, my daughter,
for your pleasure and as a tool for struggle,
against the weight of the world's troubles.
Take comfort in the knowledge that you are not alone.
There are many like you on the earth,
and you will be numbered among the warriors
when the great book is written.

Because I am your mother I will protect you
as I promised you in childhood.
You will walk freely on the planet,
my beloved daughter. Fear not
the lightning bolts of a Catholic god, or any other,
for I have placed my body and my soul between you and all harm.

Autobiography

She stalks me through the yellow flags.
If I look over my shoulder I will catch her
striding proud, a spear in her hand.
I have such a desperate need of her —
though her courage springs
from innocence or ignorance. I could lie with her
in the shade of the poplars, curled
to a foetal dream on her lap, suck
from her milk of fire to enable me fly.
Her face is my own face unblemished;
her eyes seapools, reflecting lichen,
thundercloud; her pelt like watered silk
is golden. She guides me to healing herbs
at meadow edges. She does not speak
in any tongue I recognise.
She is mother to me,
young enough to be my daughter.

The other one waits in gloomy hedges.
She pounces at night. She knows I've no choice.
She says: 'I am your future.
Look on my neck, like a chicken's
too old for the pot; my skin moults
in papery flakes. Hear it rustle?
My eyes are the gaping wounds
of newly opened graves. Don't turn
your nose up at me, madam.
You may have need of me yet.
I am your ticket underground.'
And yes she has been suckled at my own breast.
I breathed deep of the stench of her self —
the stink of railway station urinals,

of closing-time vomit, of soup lines
and charity shops. She speaks
in a human voice and I understand.
I am mother to her, young
enough to be her daughter.

I stand in a hayfield — midday, midsummer,
my birthday. From one breast
flows the Milky Way, the starry path,
a sluggish trickle of pus from the other.
When I fly off I'll glance back
once, to see my husk sink into the grasses.
Cranesbill and loosestrife will shed
seeds over it like a blessing.

'Not alone the rue in my herb garden ...'

Not alone the rue in my herb garden
passes judgement, but the eight foot
high white foxgloves among the greys
of wormwood, santolina, lavender,
the crimson rose at our cottage door,
the peas holding for dear life to their sticks
and the smaller drowning salad stuff.
The weeds grow lush and lovely
at midsummer, honeysuckle roving
through the hawthorn: my garden
at Eslin ferociously passing judgement.

We built this soil together, husband;
barrow after barrow load of peat
sieved through an old chip strainer
and the heaps of rotted manure
pushed over frosty paths on still
midwinter days, or when an east wind
chewed at our knuckles. Cranky
of a morning when the range acted up,
we still saved wood ash and dug it in,
by Christmas laid a mulch of hay
and tucked it all up safe in beds,
turned off the light and spent the most
of January and February, the bitterest days,
at chess, or poem and story making.

You were beautiful in my father's
ravelled jumper, staring at the rain,
or painting revelations of the hag
that scared the living daylights out of me.
One canvas was blacker than

the lower pits of hell after an eternity
when even the scourging fire has gone out
and the tortured souls are silenced.

O heart of my husband, I thought,
how little have I fathomed thee,
when you went and overpainted it
on a St Brigid's Day of snow and crocuses,
with a green-eyed young fiddler,
named it *Mystery Dame with Red Hair.*

We built this garden together, husband;
germinated seeds in early spring,
gambling with a crystal dice,
moon calendars and almanacs,
risked seedlings to a late black frost,
wept at loss – but some survived
to thrive a summer of aching backs.
A festive air when the poles went up
and scarlet runners coiled along the twine.
Mornings I walked out after a shower

had tamped the dust and turned
the volume way up on birdsong,
on scent, on colour, I counted myself
the luckiest woman born, to gain such
an inland kingdom, three wild
rushy acres, edged by the Eslin
trickily looping us below the hill,
our bass line to the Shannon
and the fatal rhythm of the Atlantic swell.

I did not cast it off lightly,
the yoke of work, the years of healing,
of burying my troubled dead

with every seed committed to the earth,
judging their singular, particular needs,
nurturing them with sweat and prayer
to let the ghosts go finally from me
with every basket of the harvest
I garnered in golden light for our table,
something singing in me all the while,
a song of fate, of fortune, of a journey,
a twisty road that led away from you,
my husband of the sea-scarred eyes.

Now that I return to visit you,
abandoned gardens, abandoned husband,
abandoned cat and dog and chickens,
abandoned quilts and embroideries,
high piled books, my dusty drafts,
a life I stitched together out of love,
and we sit together by the window
in the summer light, the sculptural
clouds of June, their whimsical shadows
oblivious of the grief on our faces,
in sorrow at what we built and lost
and never will rebuild, O my friend,
do not turn on me in hatred,
do not curse the day we met.

Berlin Diary, 1991

AT THE PERGAMON

The swastika at the centre
of the terracotta plate
behind security glass
in the Pergamon Museum
looks so wholly innocent.
I try to imagine the day of the potter,
a Sumerian day in 230 BC
by the bank of the Euphrates perhaps,
the clay centring on the wheel,
the thumb brought to bear
still there in the fine ridging
at the rim. This plate —
balance of held and holding,
the cold air of the museum,
the hum of the air conditioning,
the drone of a tour guide,
and the boots, the boots, the boots
of the guard echoing. My head
begins to spin.
                    The plate
begins to spin. Swastika!
Black spinning sun of my own black pupil
thrown back from the glass. My eye
and swastika one
                    black spinning sun!

I did not plan it but the clothes I chose that morning for the damp day that's in it — long navy overcoat, grey silk headscarf, and in my left ear a blue stone — makes me look like a Turkish woman.

And I am bound for the Turkish market at Kreuzberg. On the U-Bahn and the S-Bahn and the trams, so many graffiti swastikas my eyes are aching. I break my journey at Rosa Luxembourg Platz because I like the name.

A man up a ladder is postering over a street sign: Carrot Street. Carrot Street? I ask why. *All names Communist gone with the Wall.* There will be Cabbage Street and Turnip Street and Rutabaga Street and Gherkin Street.

I have no gift to bring home to my friend, and the mist is thickening and night coming on. I come to a U-Bahn. I ask directions to Kreuzberg. The man behind the counter nearly spits in my face. Misdirects me. I've a three mile walk along the canal: the lindens, the odd citizen walking a dog, a gang of mean looking youths, all looming out of the mist.

I am considering the nature of betrayal and the circumstances in an Izmir bazaar, his eye suddenly caught by the blue luminescence of the stone that now adorns my left ear. *The sign of one who's chosen the path of the warrior rather than the path of the lover,* he said when he gave it to me.

I'm trying to work all this out in iambic, trying to find the strong steady pulse of my walkabout in words. But there's too much danger at the edges, and I need all my concentration for reading the street. Visibility is down to a few yards and I've no way of knowing what will come at me next out of the mist. Another gang could materialize; or the same gang from twenty minutes ago could be coming back to get me having only now processed the signals of my garb.

When my friend gave me the earring he said it reminded him of the Miraculous Medal his mother used pin on his gansy when he was a boy, and followed it with a long rigmarole on Mariology, Earth goddesses, the power of the female, mid-Eastern moon worship, blue as a healing colour, as Mary's colour.

When I finally find the market they are packing up their wares. I choose a jet and gold anklet. I pay the jewel hawker the marks I owe her and she wraps it up. A blue stone glitters at her throat, another on her baby's blanket. *Good luck*, she says, *and health to wear it.*

HANDMADE

Your manifesto on my body
the yellow bruise on my breast
the exact same colour as the willow
at my window on Majakowskiring.

A DIFFERENT EDEN

The morning I left Dublin you were telling me a story —
a suppressed genesis. How Lilith
who pre-dated Eve went about the garden
and asked each creature, each plant,
to tell her its original name.
I pictured her stooped to a mandrake. *Mandragora officinarum.*
What the plant said to her,
or she to it for that matter, is a mystery.

We call things by their given names
as I imagine Adam meant for us to do
strutting round the garden —
You Giraffe! Me God'sman! and poor
spare-ribbed Eve tempted
by the snake totem of her wiser sister
gets them shagged into the wilderness.

A young man falls in love with Truth and searches the wide world for her. He finds her in a small house, in a clearing, in a forest. She is old and stooped. He swears himself to her service — to chop wood, to carry water, to collect the root, the stem, the leaf, the flowering top, the seed of each plant she needs for her work.

Years go by. One day the young man wakes up longing for a child. He goes to the old woman and asks to be released from his oath so that he may return to the world. *Certainly*, she says, *but on one condition: you must tell them that I am young and that I am beautiful.*

WHAT I SAW ON STARGARTENSTRASSE

Smokestack, shunting train,
cobbles scored where
her high heels have graven
ghost music in the mist.
I'm searching for my mother
after another war.

She was broody, like Sophie,
a golden hen in a story she'd tell me
to keep the nightmares away.

Ghost music on Stargartenstrasse
her high heels fragmenting cobbles,
my golden broody hen.

Oak leaves trodden to dust,
the army marches past
smokestack, shunting train.
We'll not pass this way again.

The Russian Doll

Her colours caught my eye
mixed by the light of a far off sun:
carmine, turmeric, indigo, purple —
they promised to spell us dry weather.

I'd a fiver in my pocket; that's
all they asked for. And gift wrapped her.
It had been grey all month and damp.
We felt every year in our bones

and our dead had been too much with us.
January almost over. Bitter.
I carried her home like a Holy Fire
the seven miles from the town,

my face to a wind from the north. Saw
the first primroses in the maw of a fallen oak.
There was smoke from the chimney
when I came through the woods

and though I had spent the dinner,
I knew you'd love your gaudy doll,
you'd love what's in her
at the end of your seventh winter.

The Wounded Child

1

First – gird yourself. Put on
a talisman. It may be precious
metal or common stone.

What matters is you believe
it powerful, ensurer of
a protective zone to ward off evil,

what matters is *baraka*
from years of kindly use; or that it be
 a token of a good time, like a

night under a lucky star,
untroubled, with a gentle man
who means you no harm,

or a ring given in friendship —
a calm room, maybe spring,
the light spinning out, you sip

tea and talk long into darkness
of old lives and dreamtimes,
journeys that brought you near bliss.

2

Whatever you wear you'll be strange.
This is battledress. Paint your face,
put feathers in your hair, arrange
your skirts, your skins, your lace.

Your own eyes stare out clear,
unfazed, from the bedroom mirror.
Though the mask is not familiar
your own eyes stare out. With no fear.

You are able for this.

3

Somewhere in the girl you once were
is the wounded child. Find her.
You have to find her.

She is lonely. Terrified. Curled
to a foetal grip in a tight place,
sobbing her heart out. The world

is a man with big hands
and sharp teeth. The world
is a ton of bricks, sand

in her mouth, a huge weight
on her chest. She has no breath
to speak of it. Her fate

is unwritten, silent, mute.
Remember her? Remember
her splitting apart. Tell her truth.

4

Pick her up. *Go on!*
Hold her close to you.
Hold her to your breast.
If you cannot find the words
at first, hum the tune.
They will come eventually;
like a spell or a prayer
they are already there.

When she has quietened
tell her the story of the Russian doll:

A child, lost in a forest, curls in the lip of a fallen birch among
fern and moss. She sleeps. Dreams of her mother. She clutches a
wooden doll. The woodcutter draws near. She hears beat of axe,
saw's clean song. Freed of bole, of branches, the stump swings
back, closes over her like a great mouth. And still she dreams,
opening doll after doll, seeking the kernel carved from birch
heartwood, seeking the smallest doll she can hold in her palm.
Fire consumes the forest; smoke obscures the sun. Deer and wolf
alike flee the hungry tongues. A birch seedling thrives on the spot,
thrives through the seasons until it is the finest sapling in the for-
est. The girl pushes through rings, sheds silver bark on the snow.
The yellow years fall, ripple out forever. Passing, you might hear
her voice and name it *Wind-in-Leaves*. Your heart would ache with
loneliness. She dreams of nut within shell, scrolls back to birth of
glacier, forward to death of sun. The woodcutter finds her pliant
to the whim of the wind. She surrenders to beat of axe, to saw's
clean song, welcomes the familiar refrain.

5

When your story is told
give her the Russian doll.
Make her peel away layer after layer
till she gains the inmost figure
from the birch's heartwood whittled
so small the face has lost its human guise.
Say: *Take this in your fist, love,*
grip tight and feel
glacier grind mountain to dust,
fire gallop across the taiga,
sunlight pulse through your leaves,
snow melt to nourish your roots;
bend with grace before the wind's might,
embrace beat of axe, saw's clean song.

Rescue the child

                    from her dark spell!

Rescue the child

                    from her dark spell!

Rescue the child.

25 February 1992

Island Burial

They bury their dead as quick as they can
before the shapechanging shames them
and gets them branded as witches.
I know a family had to watch their dead daughter
turn into a hare before their eyes.
They coffined her quick but swear
they heard paws against the coffin lid
as they lowered her down, as the clay fell.

SONG OF THE GRAVE

I am the grave waiting
patient receptive damp
for my hare girl in flux

when she's entered her hare self
I'll close like a fist
an end to her thumping rut

a long time hence
when you prise open my fingers
her bones on my palm

know I have cherished her

PRAYER AT THE GRAVESIDE

Burying our dead
Flesh to dust
Dust on the wind
Ash on your brow
Song of the yew
Chalice of darkness

HOW THE CHILDREN TELL IT

hare field witch
burning hare crack
cloud sea rock
a bye long sleep

hare lope green
path gate stream
sun white stone
belly breath come

hare heron cry
sand grain star
foot before foot
up stony road

hare paws hare
paws beat on wood
hare spent kick
blue eye watch

knife rope cut
home safe feather

Dream Filter

Before you were born,
I made a dream filter
to ensure you clear dreamings

for the whole of your childhood,
to the exact specifications
of a tribe I read about

in *National Geographic*. First
I'd to clear my own dreams
and pass all my bad visions

into stones; then go on foot
to pure swift running water
near where it entered the sea

and cast each weighted stone
to the pebbly bed
where they could be washed to a calm

stonedness again. Only
then was I fit to begin.

The finding of coppiced hazel,
the twisting of hempen twine,
the building of the dream filter

itself, took a full seven months.
Wait for a bird
to gift you some feathers.

on the walk to the hospital
down by the South Docks,
after a night spent in labour,

three slate-grey feathers there in my path.
I looked up and saw
a peregrine falcon hung in the air —

one of a pair that were nesting
on top of the gasometer.

This contraption
made of hazel and hemp
and a few tail feathers

is fixed tonight above your cradle.
One day you'll ask
what it's all about.

And what can I tell you?
What can I possibly say?

Birthday Present

When your father came for you
the month you turned four
you were deep in the woods with the goat.

I told him the wolves had carried you off
and left me alone.

His hands made me lie:
his soft white hands,
his short lifeline,
and what I read of his fate.

Blessing

for Tony Curtis

Not to the colony for artists
not to the walled university
but to the demented asylum
I'll go when the moon is up
in the day sky, I'll go

and snatch a song from a stranger's mouth.

They have been speaking so long
in riddles, they teach you
the heart for a child breaking,
the heart breaking for a child
is nothing more than a shift
of light on a slate roof
after rain, and the elderberry's
purpling shade is as much
as you'll know of grieving.

They have been speaking so long
in riddles the world believes at last
in enigma, the earth understands
her beguiling work —
    leaf, stone, wave.

To the demented asylum I'll go
for succour from a stranger's mouth:
    leaf crown you
        wave repeat you
            stone secure your grave

Home

I am the blind woman finding her way home by a map of tune.
When the song that is in me is the song I hear from the world
I'll be home. It's not written down and I don't remember the words.
I know when I hear it I'll have made it myself. I'll be home.

A version I heard once in Leitrim was close, a wet Tuesday night
in the Sean Relig bar. I had come for the session, I stayed
for the vision and lore. The landlord called time,
the music dried up, the grace notes were pitched to the dark.
When the jukebox blared out *I'd only four senses and he left me
    senseless,*
I'd no choice but to take to the road. On Grafton Street in
    November
I heard a mighty sound: a travelling man with a digeridoo
blew me clear to Botany Bay. The tune too far back to live in
but scribed on my bones. In a past life I may have been Kangaroo,
rocked in my dreamtime, convict ships coming o'er the foam.

In the Puzzle Factory one winter I was sure I was home.
The talking in tongues, the riddles, the rhymes, struck a chord
that cut through the pharmaceutical haze. My rhythm catatonic,
I lulled myself back to the womb, my mother's heart
beating the drum of herself and her world. I was tricked
by her undersong, just close enough to my own. I took then
to dancing; I spun like a Dervish. I swear I heard the subtle
music of the spheres. It's no place to live, but —
out there in space, on your own hung aloft the night.
The tune was in truth a mechanical drone;
I was a pitiful monkey jigging on cue. I came back to earth
with a land, to rain on my face, to sun in my hair. And grateful too.

The wisewomen say you must live in your skin, call *it* home,
no matter how battered or broken, misused by the world, you
    can heal.
This morning a letter arrived on the nine o'clock post.
The Department of Historical Reparation and who did I blame?
The Nuns? Your Mother? The State? *Tick box provided,
we'll consider your case.* I'm burning my soapbox, I'm taking
the very next train. A citizen of nowhere, nothing to my name.

I'm on my last journey. Though my lines are all wonky
they spell me a map that makes sense. Where the song that is in me
is the song I hear from the world, I'll set down my burdens
and sleep. The spot that I lie on at last the place I'll call home.

from
Dharmakaya
(2000)

for Theo Dorgan

There is nothing you can give a poet; nothing you can take away.
— Anna Akhmatova

When you ain't got nothing, you got nothing to lose.
— Bob Dylan

At the actual moment of death, one has an overwhelming
vision of Dharmakaya, or the Primary Clear Light of Pure
Reality. It is as if the whole of existence suddenly appeared
in its absolute totality and in an entirely abstract form ...
the Dharmakaya is identical with the experiencer's own
consciousness, which has no birth and no death, and is by its
very nature the Immutable Light.
— Stanislav Grof on *The Tibetan Book of the Dead*

Dharmakaya

for Thom McGinty

When you step out into death
with a deep breath,
the last you'll ever take
in this shape,

remember the first step on the street —
the footfall and the shadow
of its fall — into silence. Breathe
slow-

ly out before the foot finds solid earth again,
before the city rain
has washed all trace
of your step away.

Remember a time in the woods, a path
you walked so gently
no twig snapped
no bird startled.

Between breath and no breath
your hands cupped your own death,
a gift, a bowl of grace
you brought home to us —

become a still pool
in the anarchic flow, the street's
unceasing carnival
of haunted and redeemed.

The View from Under the Table

was the best view and the table itself kept the sky
from falling. The world was fringed with red velvet tassels;
whatever play ran in that room the tablecloth was curtains for.
I was the audience. Listen to me laughing. Listen
to me weeping. I was a child. What did I know?

Except that the moon was a porcelain globe and swung from a
    brass chain. O
that wasn't the moon at all. The moon was my true love. Oak was
    my roof and
under the table no one could see you. My granny could see me.
Out, she'd say. Out. And up on her lap the smell of kitchen and
    sleep.
She'd rock me. She'd lull me. No one was kinder.

What ails you child? I never told her. Not
one word would cross my lips. Shadows I'd say. I don't like the
    shadows.
They're waiting to snatch me. There at the turn of the stairs.
On the landing. To the right of the wardrobe. In the fridge, white
    ghosts.
Black ghosts in the coal shed. In the bread bin, hungry ghosts.

Somewhere, elsewhere, my mother was sulking in the rain. I call up
her young face. Who did she think she was with her big words
and her belt and her beatings? Who do I think I am to write her?
She must have been sad. She must have been lonely.
Discipline. Chastisement. I stretch out my four year old hands.

Fist

If this poem, like most that I write,
is a way of going back into a past
I cannot live with and by transforming that past
change the future of it, the now
of my day at the window watching
the coming and goings to Merrion Square,
then, when you present your hand to me
as fist, as threat, as weapon,
the journey back to find the hand of the little child,
the cupping of her balled fist
in my own two adult hands,
the grip of her fury, the pulse at her wrist
under the thin thin skin,
the prising loose of each hot finger
like the slow enumeration of the points of death
and the exact spot that I will have kissed
where the fate line meets the heart line —
my bloody mouth a rose suddenly blooming,
that journey takes all my strength
and hope, just as this poem does
which I present to you now.

Look! It's spread wide open in a precise
gesture of giving, of welcome,
its fate clear and empty, like the sky,
like the blue blue sky, above the Square.

That Night There Was a Full Moon, Little Cloud

Granny's up late and she's hemming her shroud.
The run and fell of it, the seemingly
seamless kilter of the over halter
that she'll slap or dash, again biting in
with what's left of her teeth. After the tea
she'll read my leaves and though the voice falters
the vision's crystal. She knows my black sin

my deep delved delight in the self same
sin. I exult in it. A lump of coal
on a white linen tablecloth — *my soul :*
a picture of it, my granny says. My name

should be harlot or scarlet. I am doomed.
She sees. She tells me I am beautiful.
That I'll never have children, but a song
for every child I might have had and none
got easy but writ in the blood of men
who've displeased me. She swears it's true. No room
of my own till the grave. The moon's strong pull
will claim me as daughter. No blame. No wrong.

Take a Breath, Hold It, Let It Go

The garden again. Finglas.
My younger sister on the coalshed roof playing circus.

Early June — elderblossom, sweet pea.
The morning carries the smell of the sea.

I'm above in the boxroom looking down at her
through the window. Eldest daughter

packing what will fit in a rucksack,
what of seventeen years I can hoist on my back.

I don't know where I'm going. She steps out
on the narrow breeze block fence. If I shout

I'll startle her. She'll fall.
I swallow back a warning, the call

of her name become a lump in my throat,
something stuck there all these years, a growth

I've tried to bawl out, dance out, weep.
The inarticulate foolish gestures of grief.

She falls anyway. I could not save her.
Then or now. My younger sister

stepping out, her tongue between her teeth,
a rapt concentration that stills the world beneath her feet.

I hold my breath. A sequinned leotard,
her velvet slippers, a cast-off battered

umbrella for balance. The spotlight blinds her,
the crowd is hushed, the tiger

paces his cage, the ringmaster
idly flicks at a fly with his whip. She falters.

I hold my breath. She finds her centre.
Then or now, I could not save her.

My Sister Lets Down Her Hair

into the winter bedroom and I turn
to the hollow of the bed we share,
her warmth still there and her smell.

It is coming on seven and she moves
by touch to her dressing. I know
every move of her and follow
her every move by the lamp of her golden hair.
As it was yesterday, and the day before,
so shall it be now in memory
a prayer for her going forth.

                     Back then,
we are lit in the cold morning by only
her rivery hair, the strong flow of her hair,
in the mirror her golden hair. The little
clouds of our breath eddy across the room
to the further shore of the window
giving on gardens and sheds. She keeps
an eye for the factory bus. Its lights
probing the room at last, she'll pick
up her bag and go from the house
without disturbing a soul.

I shift into her spot in the bed, an animal's lair,
lined with dreams and the smell of her hair,
till the dawn comes up with its clear, or its cloudy, light
wishing her back to haunt the day
with her rivery hair, her golden hair,
and I am any creature left for lonely.

My Father's Hands That Winter

That year there was cold like no other winter.
Every morning
going out was a gymnastic affair.

Even the steps inside
the house, nearly to the door
of our flat on the third floor were iced

over. Mrs. Mac broke a leg
and Harry Styx (for the first time in his life he said)
found it much too hard to beg.

We became technicians of the slide
and forward propulsion,
of throwing your body, arms wide

open, out into some zone of contract
with the air, where coming to a stop
ever ever again was taken on trust.

The city looked good enough to eat
and *weathervane* was a new word
I picked up from a storybook. Our feet

were always wet and numb and blue.

It's why I remember my father's hands so clearly.
He was out of work. It must have been through

desperation on the cusp of Christmas that he took
a job in Carton's as a turkey plucker.
For buttons, he said, and I saw a frock

like the girl's in the storybook, all fuddy duddy
in ribbons and flounces with black patent shoes.
His hands were swollen, scratched raw and bloody

from the sharp ends of feather, of sinew,
of tendon, from the fourteen-hour day,
from the bite of the boss. At the window

I'd watch each morning, impatient for dawn
and ice engineering. He'd boil up
a big pot of eggs, school lunch for us children.

He'd button down the younger ones' coats
gingerly, and tie up the laces of their shoes
and tuck in our scarves at our delicate throats

— an egg in each pocket to keep us warm,
old socks on our hands to guard against chilblains.
A kiss on his forehead to keep him from harm.

The city must have thawed at last
and unmagicked that winter when
I reached the age of reason. The past

was a new territory I would explore
at leisure and at will
by pushing on the unlatched tenement door.

I could hold in mind forever now
my father's hands that winter and
the city walls and railings freaked with snow.

The Exact Moment I Became a Poet

for Kay Foran

was in 1963 when Miss Shannon
rapping the duster on the easel's peg
half obscured by a cloud of chalk

said *Attend to your books, girls,*
or mark my words, you'll end up
in the sewing factory.

It wasn't just that some of the girls'
mothers worked in the sewing factory
or even that my own aunt did,

and many neighbours, but
that those words 'end up' robbed
the labour of its dignity.

Not that I knew it then,
not in those words — labour, dignity.
That's all back construction,

making sense; allowing also
the teacher was right
and no one knows it like I do myself.

But: I *saw* them: mothers, aunts and neighbours
trussed like chickens
on a conveyor belt,

getting sewn up the way my granny
sewed the sage and onion stuffing
in the birds.

Words could pluck you,
leave you naked,
your lovely shiny feathers all gone.

The Lost Children of the Inner City

MOLLY MALONE

Out of the debris of history
a song, a name,
a life we piece together

from odds and ends,
the cast off, the abandoned,
the lost, the useless, the relicts.

She died of a fever
the urge to save her
the same urge to gather

up the broken and the maimed
and what remains
after: a song, a name

and tokens of the sea
salty as life blood, as tears
she is moved to

though cast in bronze now
her unafflicted gaze
on the citizens who praised her

and raised her aloft
who are blind as her own bronze eyes
to the world of her children.

PRAY FOR US

Pray for us who have lost our wings
Pray for us who are broken

Pray for us whose children are cold under clay
Or swept to sea on the wind

Pray for us who live in darkness
Pray for us who die in darkness

Our children were our song
Our song is over

We are dumb with grief
Pray for us who have lost our wings

THE STONE FACES OF DUBLIN

Somewhere in the stone
was a smile, a curious gaze;

somewhere in the stone
was a human face;

somewhere in the stone
was a wink and a nod;

somewhere in the stone
was the labourer and the hod.

The mason found the gesture
like the sky when dark finds a star.

HISTORY LESSON

We read our city like an open book —
who was taken and what was took.

Spelt out in brick and mortar,
a history lesson for every mother's daughter.

Who owns which and who owns what?
The devil owns the bleeding lot!

GRANDMOTHER, GESTURE

My grandmother's hands come back to soothe me.
They smell of rain. They smell of the city.

They untangle my hair and smooth
my brow. There's more truth

to those hands than to all the poems
in the holy books. Her gesture is home.

The lines on her palms are maps:
she makes the whole world up —

she disappears it. It sings for her.
Its song is water; the sky is its colour.

She unpicks all riddles and solves
the small mysteries. She keeps the wolves

from the door. She opens wide the door.
Summer comes spilling in with a roar.

WINDOW ON THE CITY

If you blink you'd miss it,
your own life passing
into memory, frame by frame.

Sometimes you can't be sure of your own name.
So fast, the changing
face of the city. From where you sit

not the swish of the tyger's tail,
not the twitch of the tyger's whiskers
not a glance of his frisky eye

regarding: just the emptiest sky
pockets that couldn't be any lighter,
a train singing on its iron rail.

BUDDLEJA

Self-seeding, stubborn, cute,
given half a chance they root

in a hair's breadth gap in a brick,
or chimneypot. Or fallen into a crack

and left for a year they're a shrub
tough and tenacious as your indigenous Dub.

When they break into blossom — so free, so beautiful.
I name them now as flags of the people.

Ectopic

The four full moons of the yellow sky
pulsate. Four full moons and I need
morphine. I need more morphine to stop the hurting.

I would gut my granny for another hit.
Someone's sewn me up and left the kitchen tap,
the apple Mac, a rabid bat, a handy anvil

inside me. The stitches there above the mons
(*Won't interfere with the bikini line ...*) neat
as my own white teeth clenched and grinding in pain,

that grin up, second mouth!, at the ceiling lights, the moons! and
I will work out their complicated orbits
relative to the sun and why the stars have

all deserted me. I want to know the weight
of my little creature's soul and why its fate

has been to leave before I had a chance to save
her. Or him. It? They keep calling it *it*.
I am a woman with a sieve carrying sand

from the beach. And all this time the rain
is hammering the window pane. I count perfect feet.
Your ten perfect toes. Your perfect fingers ten. Your blue eyes, since,

perfect foetus, I must summon up the will to kill
you soon before you get too strong a grip
on the black hole that occupies the void that was my heart.

O somewhere there is a beautiful myth of sorting,
of sifting through a mountain of dross to find the one seed
whose eventual blossom is such would make a god cry.

Three Love Songs

THE COAST OF LEITRIM

On an autumn day in the hot city
blue sky and black shadow cast
to concrete and grey sward and dust, a lost
voice urges leave all the pretty

people behind, spend this equinox
walking the long and lonely coast of Leitrim.
You come too. Do. On a whim.
The way you used to, intox-

icated with me and my other, ready
to hop on a bus or a plane or a train or
any craft to share the transport, before
we grew serious and dour. *Steady,*

steady, you'd say as our heads blew off
or the sea dissolved another cliff face
or a fissure opened and swallowed us
whole. Because, my honey, you'd have to laugh

at how little stays the same. Grown
up now and no wiser than that first
time we walked the coast of Leitrim, no worst
there was none ... so delicate and unknown

to each's other, finding my own lovely coastline
as exotic as the unmapped edge of the universe
that expands rapidly to leave way too much space
between our stars. Litorally fine

as when you reached for my hand
that day, at the sea's restless edge.
In sight of two rivers you solemnly pledged
my kingdom was as much land

as I could walk: the whole coast
of Leitrim — each rock and stone of it, each cloud,
each water-loving willow and every common herb, each blade
of grass, and even every shadow that they cast.

THE BOG OF MOODS

The first time I cross the Bog of Moods
I misread the map.
The Bog of Moons I thought it was
and watched as your white cap

lifted by a sudden squall
was cast before me unto the canal
a full moon itself on the jet black water
shattering the perfect mirror

of the starry heavens. Seeds
of light prolific as common duckweed,
fen sedge, pollution-intolerant arrowhead.
Bistort. Bulrush. Bog bean. Bur-reed.

The low down belly rooted naming
of these wet toed, turf sucking
mockers at our hamfisted, clubfooted clumsy
taking of each other. Glory be to whimsy

and misreading that have us cross the Bog
of Moots or Moos. For yes, they're there —
the slow moan of them squelching through the fog
of their own breaths, swinging full udders,

dainty hoofs picking through bladderwort
and crowfoot. Hells bells! And helleborine!
The harder you look, the more you will have seen;
and I say forgive me for the tense and curt

way I've been all day. The world
had shrunk to the proportion of the narrowboat.
I was a termagant curled
in the prickly armour of my pre-menstrual overcoat

barking at the moon, the mood,
the moot, the moos, until the moment when we stood
hand in hand under the stars and you showed me the rare
and lovely Grass of Parnassus, far

from its usual habitat. And something loosened
and came right, as if the land
herself was settling down, plumping out her skirts,
prepared to take her ease, and done with birth.

AT SLYGUFF LOCK

You whisper sweet nothings to my chilled ear.
The boat rocks; the wind swings round the compass
and drops the wild plums to the ground. I fear
the storm will break the ties and turn us loose

on the river's floodwater that carries
wrenched trees; galvanised sheets; plastic bottles;
one sheep's carcass, its face full of worries.
You ask I listen — the river's glottals

in duet now with canalwater's fall.
It drowns out even my own heart thumping,
the thock of the boat on the granite wall,
the insidious *chunka* of chains bumping.

All this to do about nothing, sweetheart.
With each falling leaf, a spark of god'sfire
singeing the earth where it falls. O the chart
to these waters says nothing about air

(for its long repeat makes the pattern hard
to map), and water is faster than stone,
and mountains are slowest of all — they ward
off the fickle, the inconstant. They hone

themselves in pure air, which element tonight
is ours to shine in, while the river sobs
its long song of courtship to the moon's bright
face; sheltering near us, a swan and her cob.

The Tantric Master

For I shall consider his beautiful navel firstly
— an altar! — whereat I've often offered flowers,
the yellow buttercup especially, a monstrance I can elevate
to the memory of his mother who surely taught him to pet.
And honeysuckle and meadowsweet and the wild dog rose:
one for its scent, one for its sound, and one for the tone of his skin
that is all petal to me.
             For I shall consider
secondly each individuated pore of his entire body
and consider each at length having nothing better
to do with my time, and each being a universe unto itself.
This I call rapture.
             And thirdly, to make no bones
about it, being the crux, the hardest part of the matter,
I shall consider his noble and magical wand. He do good
business throughout the night with it. He enchant,
and spellbind and wind me round his little finger;
or, on a moony night in April, even his little toe.

Which brings me to his nails: he keepeth that trim and smooth
the better to pleasure me. So subtle his touch I can feel
the very whorls of his fingerprints and could reconstruct from
    memory
his mark on my breast. Each ridge the high mountain,
each trough the deep canyon, unfathomable;
but I, having buckets of time, do fathom, do fathom.

For I shall consider the mesmeric draw of his nipples,
like standing stone circles on the broad plain of his chest,
megalithic power spots when I lay my hot cheek
on the cool of his belly and sight through the meadows
and the distant forests the trajectory of sun and other stars.

His mouth, I won't go into, being all cliché in the face of it ,
except to say the dip of his lip is most suited to suction and friction,
and other words ending in tion, tion, tion, which come to think of it
when I'm in the grip of it, is exactly how I make sweet moan.
                    For I shall consider
him whizzbang dynamo and hellbent on improving my spiritual
    status.

You can keep your third eyes and your orbs sanctimonious
the opening of which my Master believes *is* the point.
He says I'm a natural and ultimate enlightenment a mere question
    of time.
But in patient devotion I'll admit to deficiency. The theory of being
not a patch on just being is. Yap I distrust! Show me.
Don't tell me the way. The right place for talk of this ilk
is not during, not after, and foretalk will get you nowhere at all.
The best that I hope for in our daily instructions
is the lull between breaths, spent and near pacified.

Suburb

DESIRE PATH

For days before the kids were gathering stuff —
pallets and cast-off furniture, the innards of sheds,
the guts of Barna huts. Local factories on red alert
for raiding parties under cover of dark.

I watched them lug and drag fair-got and knocked-off
gear across the park, to the gap in the hedge,
to their deep ditched hoarding spot where they kept
it dry and guarded against the rival gang's attack.

They reminded me of bees, making to the flower
or worker ants. Their comings and goings wore

the grass away until there was only bare earth
on their preferred track — a desire path

inscribed on the sward. I reckon seen from above
it must look umbilical to some object of exotic love.

STOOD UP

Leaning against the tree for over an hour,
young man waiting — for his girl, I assume.
All Souls' Day and the leaves falling dreamily.
I've seen the girl he's waiting for, a flirt,

up at the pub with the shiny gang, a short time
ago. Skulling pints. She's having a baby.
At least that's the word out there on the street.
They say it's not his. The first day of winter

is sweet and mild and gold and blue. He looks
beyond the aspen's tremulous leaf
to where small children fan the embers

of last night's bonfire. They coax a flame. It sucks
the air vigorously, then hesitates, then takes like grief
that's easier borne now than it will be to remember.

PYROLATRY

'Our wheelie bin was missing after the bin collection today.
It has no. 13 painted in white on one side.
If you happen to see it, please let us know.'
Should I tell them about the flames I saw

earlier — the green and the purple and the blue. The way
they snaked and writhed, sometimes narrow, sometimes wide,
could only have been plastic, toxic and noxious, so
strong the smell on the breeze. I had to claw

the washing in, which hung for hours in Virgo
from the drying line, which reeled and jigged
through that constellation until dark fell

and the wind dropped its poisoned cargo.
The flames veered east, then north, the kids ligged
round; then someone turned up with a drum — autumn's knell.

STINK BOMB

The smell of which still hangs about the house
despite the scented candles, the essential oils
I've burned and censered through the rooms
like a priestess in a diabolic rite.

Of course the row we had could have roused
the undead and the dead alike. It left me coiled
in a foetal crouch behind the couch, some womb
I was trying to get back to. And shite

if we didn't wake next door's dog; the Hound from Hell
Himself right on cue. You'd have to laugh. Or die
trying. Between your irrefutable logic

and my inarticulate sobs, we missed the door bell
ringing, we missed the children singing *trick
or treat, trick or treat, the ghost afloat, the witch afly.*

MISTLE THRUSH

The sycamore is weeping leaves of fire;
a maple stands in its own flaming lake;
shy birches isolate in yellow puddles.
You'd half expect these young trees to kick

their fallen skirts away. Bride? Bullfighter?
Dervish dancer rapt in a swirling cape?
When I went out an hour ago to muddle
through the leafdrift at my door, a flock

of mistle thrush descended — a deputation
from the wingéd world with urgent and with fatal news:
Dying is simple. You breathe in, you breathe out, you breathe in,
you breathe out and you don't breathe in again.
They acted like this was cause for celebration
— the first minor chord of my winter blues.

SUDDEN RAIN

I'm no Buddhist: too attached to the world.
of my six senses. So in this unexpected shower.
I lift my face to its restorative tattoo
the exultation of its anvil chime on leaf.

On my tongue I taste the bitter city furled
in each raindrop; and through the sheeted fall of grief
the glittery estate doth like a garment wear
the beauty of the morning; the sweet reek of miso

leached from composting leaves. Last night's dream
of a small man who floated in the branches of an oak
harvesting mistletoe with a golden sickle

I intuit as meaning you'll be tender and never fickle
this winter, though this may be synaesthetic
nonsense; I've little left to go on, it would seem.

MALICE AFORETHOUGHT

Her tongue would flense the flesh from off your back.
I've never heard her utter a good word
about a neighbour or a friend in need.
Yet half the time you'd listen to spite your self,
knowing full well tomorrow it's your turn
to squirm and be lambasted on the spit,
the faggots stacked about your feet, the match

struck and held to straw and twigs. Should it catch
and take — the whole estate is lit
in the glare and glamour, while the one who burns
discovers the heft of our black craft, our art, frail shell.
Each flaming word a falling leaf — seed
nurturer and comforter that'll one day lift a bird
from the earth to its nest, a worm in its beak.

Literacy Class, South Inner City

for Ursula Coleman

One remembers welts festering on her palm.
She'd spelt 'sacrament' wrong. Seven years of age,
preparing for Holy Communion. Another is calm
describing the exact humiliation, forty years on, the rage

at wearing her knickers on her head one interminable day
for the crime of wetting herself. Another swears she was punch
    drunk
most her schooldays — clattered about the ears, made to say
I am stupid; my head's a sieve. I don't know how to think.

I don't deserve to live.
                    Late November, the dark
chill of the room, Christmas looming and none of us well fixed.
We bend each evening in scarves and coats to the work
of mending what is broken in us. Without tricks,

without wiles, with no time to waste now, we plant
words on these blank fields. It is an unmapped world
and we are pioneering agronomists launched onto this strange
    planet,
the sad flag of the home place newly unfurled.

The Trapped Woman of the Internet

She turns to me or any other watcher
her freaked almond eyes: I imagine she says
rescue me, rescue me. And the only
rescue I can mount is to shift website
from Asiatic Babe Cutie Triple XXX Sexpot.
Yet much as I want I cannot leave her
rest. She bothers me all the mundane livelong day.
I carry her to the edges of my own lonely
room, and in the coldest hour of this winter's night
I lay her down upon a fragrant cot

of dried meadow grasses, strewing herbs,
and off her thin and pallid face
I sponge the thick and viscid stuff;
and at this point before the fire, I have to curb
such useless gesture towards an empty space
where no one can be saved, or loved enough

to save ourselves from our own virtual childhoods,
to puzzle ourselves free from those enchanted woods.

Swallows and Willows

When he caught me at the corner
with the curly headed green eyed boy
he brought me into detention.

'Write out, let me see,
a verse of a poem. Any
verse of your choice,

but longer than a quatrain,
five lines at least.
A hundred times.'

>   *from* The Jailer (underlined three times)
>   by Sylvia Plath

>   *I imagine him*
>   *Impotent as distant thunder,*
>   *In whose shadow I have eaten my ghost ration.*
>   *I wish him dead or away.*
>   *That, it seems, is the impossibility.*

I was neat at first, maybe
neat to the tenth time, then
a looping downward scrawl.

Out the window — swallows
and willows and sun on the river.
'I meant a verse from a *set* text.'

I sat at the edge of his class
right into summer exams
sulky, and lonely, and cruel.

In Memory, John Borrowman

All things move through me:
the wind that shakes the willow;
my old friend's last breath.

On Poetry

for Niamh Morris

VIRGIN

To look back then:
one particular moon snared in the willows
and there I am sleeping in my body,
a notebook beside me with girl poems in it
and many blank pages to fill
and let there be a rose and the memory of its thorn
and a scar on my thigh where the thorn had ripped

earlier that day in the abandoned garden
where he came first to me
and lifted my skirt
and we sank to the ground.

And let me be peaceful
for I wasn't.
Not then, not for many moons after.

MOTHER

mother you terrorist
muck mother mud mother
you chewed me up
you spat me out

mother you devourer
plucker of my soul bird
mammal self abuser
nightmatrix huntress

mother keeper
of calender and keys
ticking off moon days
locking up the grain

mother house and tomb
your two breasts storing
strontium and lies
when you created time

mother you created plenty
you and your serpent consort
you and your nests
you and your alphabets

mother your pictographs
your mandalas your runes
your inches your seconds
your logic your grammar

mother wearing a necklace of skulls
who calls into being
by uttering the name
mater logos metric

mother your skirts
your skins your pelts
with your charms
old cow I'm your calf

mother fetishist
heart breaker
forsaker and fool
in the pouring rain

mother I stand
over your grave
and your granite headstone
and I weep

WHORE

I learnt it well. I learnt it early on:
that nothing's free, that everything is priced
and easier do the business, be cute, be wized
up and sussed, commodify the fun

than barter flesh in incremental spite
the way the goodwives/girlfriends did
pretending to be meek and do as bid
while close-managing their menfolk. It wasn't right.

I believed it wasn't right. See me now -
I'm old and blind and past my sexual prime
and it's been such a long and lonely time
since I felt fire in my belly. I must allow

there'll be no chance of kindling from my trance
the spark that wakes the body into dance;
yet still comes unbidden like god's gift: an image —
a boy turns beneath me, consolatory and strange.

Recovery

The gardener is sweeping
the moss garden free
of the fallen husks of moss blossom
and other debris

that the wild wind dumped on it.
Such careful work
on such a small scale.
She loosens up the rich loam with a fork.

Her brow bowed to the ground
down on her knees there —
no time, and all time
to work this gently on the earth.

I have been bad all winter
and dreamt through last night's bitter cold
that this is my final spring —
the first green still cased in gold.

The gardener is so delicate,
each gesture a sure touch,
as if she were painting a miniature landscape
with her bristle brush.

I could watch her forever
at her patient sweeping.
Across the valley, in the state forest, the crew
are trail blazing.

Though I cannot see them
I have heard since dawn

at the very edge of my world
the whine of their machines.

I want to be like her. To take care
of the garden, to sweep clear a bed
of the deepest, greenest moss,
to recover a mossy pillow for my weary head.

It is All I Ever Wanted

for Eavan Boland

to sit by this window
the long stretched light of April falling
on my desk, to allow

the peace of this empty page
and nearing
forty years of age

to hold in these hands
that have learnt to be soothing
my native city, its hinterland

and backstreets and river scored
memory of spring
blossom and birds —

my girl-poems
fountaining
over grief and the want of someplace to call home.

Last week I took as metaphor, or at least as sign,
a strange meeting:
a young fox walking the centre line

down the south side of the Square
at three in the morning.
She looked me clear

in the eyes, both of us curious
and unafraid. She was saying —
or I needed her to say — *out of the spurious*

the real, be sure
to know the value of the song
as well as the song's true nature.

Be sure, my granny used say,
of what you're wanting,
for fear you'd get it entirely.

Be sure, I tell myself,
you are suffering
animal like the fox, not nymph

nor sylph, nor figment,
but human heart breaking
in the silence of the street.

Familiar who grants me the freedom of the city,
my own hands spanning
the limits of pity.

from

Painting Rain

(2009)

for Eavan Boland

Words cannot express Truth.
That which words express is not Truth.
— The Diamond Sutra

The mysteries of the forest disappear with the forest.
— Theo Dorgan

Death of a Field

The field itself is lost the morning it becomes a site
When the Notice goes up: Fingal County Council — 44 units

The memory of the field is lost with the loss of its herbs

Though the woodpigeons in the willow
The finches in what's left of the hawthorn hedge
And the wagtail in the elder
Sing on their hungry summer song

The magpies sound like flying castanets

And the memory of the field disappears with its flora:
Who can know the yearning of yarrow
Or the plight of the scarlet pimpernel
Whose true colour is orange?

The end of the field is the end of the hidey holes
Where first smokes, first tokes, first gropes
Were had to the scentless mayweed

The end of the field as we know it is the start of the estate
The site to be planted with houses each two or three bedroom
Nest of sorrow and chemical, cargo of joy

The end of dandelion is the start of Flash
The end of dock is the start of Pledge
The end of teazel is the start of Ariel
The end of primrose is the start of Brillo
The end of thistle is the start of Bounce
The end of sloe is the start of Oxyaction
The end of herb robert is the start of Brasso
The end of eyebright is the start of Persil

Who amongst us is able to number the end of grasses
To number the losses of each seeding head?

                            I'll walk out once
Barefoot under the moon to know the field
Through the soles of my feet to hear
The myriad leaf lives green and singing
The million million cycles of being in wing

That — before the field become map memory
In some archive on some architect's screen
I might possess it or it possess me
Through its night dew, its moon white caul
Its slick and shine and its profligacy
In every wingbeat in every beat of time

Not Weeding

Nettle, bramble, shepherd's purse —
refugees from the building site
that was once the back field,

my former sworn enemies
these emissaries of the wild
now cherished guests.

Tanka

When he stepped ashore
his eyes were the deepest green
as if he dreamt leaves
across the wide Atlantic
to reel him home to Ireland.

Opening his book
I wrote — the wake of bristle
barely dipped in ink
that brushed on dampened paper,
invites a poem pool to light

through the pulse beating
wane of the moon, as land ebbs
from him, the tide line
washing clean the page's span,
making fast the boat — the stars

that brought him back safe
shine further into night skies
wheeling overhead
in a new constellation
less finned nor furred than feathered.

This coming winter
he will dream the vast ocean
back into his eyes.
The morning he'll rise to leave
his eyes will be deepest blue.

Deadwood

Me with the secateurs, you with the Greek saw;
we cut the creeper back, we prune the rose;
cotoneaster and privet get the chop —
more on the compost heap than left on hedge.

The walls look cold, naked; the shrubbery raw
and wounded where we snip. We trust it grows
back. You're stuck up the ladder reaching to lop
off a cankerous branch. Your tool's honed edge

whines as it goes. All day you lay down the law.
You'd swear you'd a PhD in pruning. God knows
I'm as bad with my cranks and my post op
critique of your handiwork; or worse — I dredge

from our primeval bed, the sea's wide floor,
my pearls of wisdom, my swinish garden lore.

At Dublin Zoo

A four-year-old
Seeing elephants
For the first time

'But they're not blue'

'She didn't know she was dying but the poems did'

for Jody Allen Randolph

She didn't know she was dying but the poems did.
They carried on as usual. They understood

that every moon was a waning moon,
each flower already past its bloom;

the city of her birth was a ghost city,
even the ghosts had exhausted her pity;

her old lovers, her mother, her lost children
were muddled into the ghost cauldron.

When she got Lough Léinn in a line
it was for the toxic algal scum, the greenish-brown

stain spreading over the surface of water
by whose shores Oisín had hunted deer

through the *ceo draíochta* that presaged Niamh.
The old language itself was a reason to grieve.

So many dying languages. Her ode to the Nushu tongue
of Central China, the last woman-specific language

as far as she could tell, which died with Yang Huanji
of Hunan Province, in her 98th year, could be

read as foreshadowing her own death.
Certainly the lines shortened, as if breath

itself was thinning, ornament sparse,
the poem a horse drawn vehicle, a hearse

clipping along, not as in wild youth the thunderous ride
bare back, white-knuckled above the thundering tide.

The poems kept the secret of her death from her:
when the mooring line went slack in the water,

and her craft began its slow drift into the light —
rudderless, the shrouds no longer taut

to the truck, the clouds a raggy flag atop the mast.
She was free to go with the current at last.

Her death belonged to the poems; they kept it
safe from her, knowing she would not accept it.

Hagiography

Just back from Éigse Michael Hartnett.
You'd have to laugh. His corpse not even cold yet.

Very aboriginal to be beneath a sign at the brand new estate:
Address — Michael Hartnett Close, Newcastle West.

Its position is perfect — right opposite Coole Lane.
Stood there in the pouring rain with his son

Across from The Healing Streams Therapy Centre,
St Vincent de Paul, within earshot of the river

On a quiet day.
                    Get this: the story Joan Mac Kernan
Told us of the poetry workshop for children

Earlier, when she asked who'd heard of Michael Hartnett,
The lad who cried 'Miss, Miss, I live in Michael Hartnett.'

I recognised the mantra
Like a glittering speck of mica

Whirling down the bardos from another incarnation
To blaze the words as the tune is spun.

All together now: I live in Michael Hartnett.
I live in Michael Hartnett. I live in Michael Hartnett.

Sea

for Tony Walsh

FROM SCRATCH

To begin again: my hands sifting sand
at the sea's edge, and nothing to be done.
All day to do it in. To start again
from scratch; a driftwood stick, a hazel wand
to scribe your name deep in the newfound land
the ebbing tide has granted me. The sun
is a time bomb tossed to the blue heaven;
clouds shadow my script, shadow my young hand.
A heron takes flight as if not knowing
yet what its own wings can do. There are reams
of Brent geese landing with their hungry song.
At the tide's edge your name — going, going
gone with the turning tide. What was mere dream
of empire — dissolved, wrecked. Gone badly wrong.

HIGH TIDE

When we stole out of the sleeping estate
down to the sea shore, we were thieves of night.
We were thieves of grief, of longing, of light.
Hand in hand, each the other's chosen mate.

We wanted to copperfasten our fate
in the sound of, in the face of, in sight
of, the highest tide either one of us might
know. We wanted to feel that mortal weight.

The neighbours must have shifted in their dreams
and turned, or sighed, or called out of their sleep
some lost love's name, some unmourned daughter's death;
as in: my Sarah, my Nancy, my Liam.
Lyric of their secret fret the sea keeps —
the drowned forever singing their last breath.

SULLEN

The islands appear, they vanish, return.
A dog worries her image in a pool;
disturbs the mirror, digs deep in the sand,
self unfathomable. And I, who learn
this craft at the expense of art: mere fool
that the sea abandons high on dry land.

HANDSEL

I take my black dog down to the winter sea;
a mere drop in the ocean each salt tear.
The north wind is bitter, threatening snow;
it whips up the waves, it whines through the dunes.
A small boat is wrecked on the rocks — dragged free
of its mooring, dismasted, all its gear
and tackle cast on the tide. A lone crow
blown from the woods caws his hooded tune
to the water.
            O the sea neither gives
nor takes as we fancy. The sea has no needs,
nor worries, nor wants. If we call it 'she' —

an ur mother — it is because salt lives
in our blood. And grief drops salt like seeds;
brings home shells in pockets — memory.

ASHES

The tide comes in; the tide goes out again
washing the beach clear of what the storm
dumped. Where there were rocks, today there is sand;
where sand yesterday, now uncovered rocks.

So I think on where her mortal remains
might reach landfall in their transmuted forms,
a year now since I cast them from my hand
— wanting to stop the inexorable clock.

She who died by her own hand cannot know
the simple love I have for what she left
behind. I could not save her. I could not
even try. I watch the way the wind blows
life into slack sail: the stress of warp against weft
lifts the stalling craft, pushes it on out.

Nomad Heart

for Kevin Page

Sometimes looking to the cold wintry stars
you can feel the planet move as it whirls
in the flux of the galaxy, the whole
path of the milky way buzzing like a hive.

They say it's better to journey than arrive —
halting being the usual rigmarole
of move-along-shift. Sometimes the soul
just craves a place to rest, safe from earthly wars.

The city lights come on in twos and threes
and leaves are freezing hard in mucky pools,
cars are stuck in jams or droning home.

If we're not brought to our knees, we'll fall to our knees
in thanks, in praise, in trust, in hope — the rule
of law mapped clear on heaven's ample dome.

Six Sycamores

The original leaseholders around St. Stephen's Green had to plant six sycamores and tend them for three years.

THE SYCAMORE'S CONTRACT WITH THE CITIZENS

To look up in autumn — the fiery crown
loosing and netting the sky by turns; the seeds
stopping time, helicoptering lazily down
to crashland on paths or on a pad of weeds

when you were a child. And imagined the birds
as the souls of the builders; their flighty shades
gossip through the years' unleaving — their words
drift slowly down the airwaves as the light fades.

To remember the planters with their common tools,
spade, rake, hoe; the forms so crafty, so good,
so sharp, so meet for the job, nobody fool
enough to try to improve on them. Dream of bud;

and earth's opening gesture to the root of the sycamore
as it probes below ground for the source of this metaphor.

09.20   FIRST SYCAMORE

a girl stops for a moment
a stone in her boot
on her Walkman Bob Dylan
he that's not busy being born is busy dying

she's late for school
she smokes a last fag

NUMBER FIFTY-ONE

And as the ages pass, the solid world longs
for its own dissolution: those red bricks
dream of the clay pit; with every lick
of the north wind rough render remembers the song

of the river grinding it down; granite quoins desire
their home in the mountains — above Ballyknockan, the wild
bird's lonely tune, the shadow on the lake;

the iron railings guard the memory of fire,
of ore-selves before being smelted and cast and exiled
to these unforgiving streets; the shutters ache

for the woods, the greeny light, the sap strong
in bole, in branch, the undergrowth quick
with life; linen drapes must crave someone to unpick,
to unspin, to be bluest flax blossom all summer long.

04.26 SECOND SYCAMORE

you couldn't take your eyes off of her
give us a break
you were looking at her all night
for the love and honour ...
you don't care about me
will you shush

you don't give a toss
you'll wake the dead
you were drooling over her
donne moi un break wagon
come back here you

NUMBER FIFTY-TWO

La Touche is in his counting house, counting out
his money. He's piling up the gold coin
in neat and shiny rows. A twinge of gout
but otherwise all well. The new house on the Green

is splendid, plasterwork sublime, furnishings divine
and Angelica Kaufmann turning up on a chance
visit. Such a boon. He'll hurry to join
her for tea before dark. He can already sense

her copy of Guido's *Aurora* is a work of immense
beauty. The way she's found in the pearly light
of a Dublin dawn the exact tone for the dance
of all that mythic flesh across his ceiling. She might

well paint the grove's tender green from those sycamores.
She's worth her weight in snotty stuccodores!

spare a few bob mister
a few bob for a cup of tea
any odds mister
spare change please
help the homeless missus
a few pence for a hostel
god bless you love
spare a few bob mister

'ALL TRADES, THEIR GEAR AND TACKLE AND TRIM'
 — *Father Hopkins*

Their kit and their rig. The beloved adze and auger,
bodkin and borer, chisel and clamp, diestock and drill,
the edgetools and files, graver, hammer, inker,
the jemmy, knives, lathe and mitre, the mill,

the nibbler; on and on in serried ranks,
the marching army of the wielders of tools.
And whether they are saints or fools
we'll raise a glass and offer thanks

to the makers and minders of our material world.
In their war against time: daemons fire them;
St. Joseph bear them; muses inspire them.
Guild banner, lodge pennant, red flag of labour unfurled!

And somewhere in the upper story the Architect
uncertain whether to dance or genuflect.

14.48 FOURTH SYCAMORE

she feels a kick in her belly
on her way to Holles Street
for the seven month check up
she steadies herself at the tree
imagining the rings within the bark
she waits for her creature to settle
her first child

THEM DUCKS DIED FOR IRELAND

> '6 of our waterfowl were killed or shot, 7 of the garden seats broken and about 300 shrubs destroyed.'
> — Park Superintendent in his report on the damage to St. Stephen's Green sustained during the Easter Rising, 1916

Time slides slowly down the sash window
puddling in light on oaken boards. The Green
is a great lung, exhaling like breath on the pane
the seasons' turn, sunset and moonset, the ebb and flow

of stars. And once made mirror to smoke and fire,
a Republic's destiny in a Countess' stride,
the bloodprice both summons and antidote to pride.
When we've licked the wounds of history, wounds of war,

we'll salute the stretcher bearer, the nurse in white,
the ones who pick up the pieces, who endure,
who live at the edge, and die there and are known

by this archival footnote read by fading light;
fragile as a breathmark on the windowpane or the gesture
of commemorating heroes in bronze and stone.

coming off the nightshift
the youth dreams of the Lotto
they can all fuck off then
the mac-boss with his mac-job
with his mac-mobile and his mac-mind
from the airport he'll text them
I resign

LIMINAL

I've always loved thresholds, the stepping over,
the shapechanging that can happen when
you jump off the edge into pure breath and then
the passage between inner and outer.

Mist becomes cloud; becomes rain. Water. Ice. Water.
In the daily flux, no telling where one will end or begin.
Death can kick start and birth be the true El Fin.
You jig and you reel through molecular spin, daughter.

Nothing can harm you or cure you. You've found
a clear path through the chaos, a loaning

from history and whether you are free or bound
is still in the balance. There's no gain in owning.

Old riddles still posit the same — what is the sound
of one hand clapping? Is that the door opening or closing?

19.38 SIXTH SYCAMORE

years later he tells her
he hid behind the tree
and watched her
sitting on granite steps
waiting for him to show
their first date
spring blossom falling like snow

In Memory, Joanne Breen

I am fingering a length of yarn
from the mill at Stornoway.
It is green as a summer meadow
though when I untwine it widdershins
I see, spun into the yarn, fibres of blue
& yellow & purple, occasionally orange.

I am undoing the magic of the spindle,
unravelling.

The day we buried her, gorse was a golden flame.

We buried the summer with her, we buried
high clouds of May, the swallows we buried —
those stitchers of land to sea, those grafters of sky
to the dark earth which opened to her beauty.

We buried the song of her body and all it promised
of betrothal & children & work: the way
she would weave dolphin & salmon & swan
in a tapestry out of the land itself,
its very warp & woof, its stuff, its dye, its fixings,
the land she trod so lightly on.

I am fingering a length of yarn
from the mill at Stornoway. Deep winter now
and the wind crying in the chimney.
The candle gutters in a draught;
the shadow sways on the wall
and breath — breath snags on memory.

Once upon a springtime she is a girl
in the branches of an old beech in the back field.
She holds fast to the rope and out she jumps —

the dog, the clouds, the hedgerows,
the rooftop, the haybarn, the cows,
the stream, the starlings, the byre,
the bees, the hill, the village,
all spun together— dizzy and giddy she laughs
swinging out into the arms of our love.

Snowdrops

So long trying to paint them, failing
to paint their shadows on the concrete path.

They are less a white than a bleaching out of green.
If you go down on your knees

and tilt their petals towards you
you'll look up under their petticoats

into a hoard of gold
like secret sunlight and their

three tiny striped green awnings that lend a
kind of frantic small-scale festive air.

It is the first day of February
and I nearly picked a bunch for you,

my dying friend, but remembered in time
how you prefer to leave them

to wither back into the earth;
how you tell me it strengthens the stock.

Cora, Auntie

Staring Death down
with a bottle of morphine in one hand,
a bottle of Jameson in the other:

laughing at Death —
love unconditional keeping her just this side
of the threshold

as her body withered
and her eyes grew darker and stranger
as her hair grew back after chemo

thick and curly as when she was a girl;
always a girl in her glance
teasing Death — humour a lance

she tilted at Death.
Scourge of Croydon tram drivers and High Street dossers
on her motorised invalid scooter

that last year:
bearing the pain,
not crucifixion but glory

in her voice.
Old skin, bag of bones,
grinning back at the rictus of Death:

always a girl in her name —
Cora, maiden, from the Greek Κορη,
promising blossom, summer, the scent of thyme.

Sequin: she is standing on the kitchen table.
She is nearly twenty one.
It is nineteen sixty one.

They are sewing red sequins, the women,
to the hem of her white satin dress
as she moves slowly round and round.

Sequins red as berries,
red as the lips of maidens,
red as blood on the snow

in Child's old ballads,
as red as this pen
on this white paper

I've snatched from the chaos
to cast these lines
at my own kitchen table —

Cora, Marie, Jacinta, my aunties,
Helena, my mother, Mary, my grandmother —
the light of those stars

only reaching me now.
I orbit the table I can barely see over.
I am under it singing.

She was weeks from taking the boat to England.
Dust on the mantelpiece,
dust on the cards she left behind:

a black cat swinging in a silver horseshoe,
a giant key to the door,
emblems of luck, of access.

All that year I hunted sequins:
roaming the house I found them
in cracks and crannies,

in the pillowcase,
under the stairs,
in a hole in the lino,

in a split in the sofa,
in a tear in the armchair
in the home of the shy mouse.

With odd beads and single earrings,
a broken charm bracelet, a glittering pin,
I gathered them into a tin box

which I open now in memory —
the coinage, the sudden glamour
of an emigrant soul.

Peter, Uncle

Think memory a river.

Back then,
as far back as I can go,
near the headwaters:

a wind tossed a seed head in
and it is carried by the current
to this muddy shore

low lying estuarial land
of Baldoyle, part gravel bank
part coastal meadow
where I reach my fiftieth year

it snags and roots and grows and blossoms —
now this flowering:

back then as far
back as I can go —

1961? '62? How old am I?
Six? Seven?

Me at the front of the scooter
standing between his knees
holding on for dear life.

Pat, my aunt, his wife-to-be, perched on the back,
off each Sunday after lunch
to look at how their house was growing

course by breezeblock course
in a field in Artane,
the city pushing out a new suburb.

The curiousness
to the solemn child I was
of Peter Field visiting a field where

he was like some god of the field,
hermetic of the thing and its name
and the blade cutting into the turf
to open the field
to let his will be done.

The house foundations were planted like crops in their neat rows
the song of cement mixers
brickies whistling in the winter air
the field itself dying as the crop matured.

That moment
when the roof went on —
what was enclosed then:
call that mystery home.

Forward: another memory
washes downriver to this estuarial backwater
for my gaze to fall on it —

me at thirteen in their kitchen,
children around us.

Peter drawing on the ember of his pipe —

look: this is how you change a fuse
are you paying attention?

He explains the flow of it —

current danger   you should know   you need to know

Who in those days would teach a girl such a thing?
Access, suddenly, knowledge.

He never gave up on me:
the family joke I became then —

pauper-poet, wandering star,
what is all this education for?
down at heel and
down at mouth and
all prickles and class anger and
always in trouble and heartbroke,
what I remember of the seventies.

He never gave up on me.

A night of rain,
such rain gurgling in the gutters
weeping in the shores
great struggling gulps of it against the rooves
sighing down the windowpanes

visiting the house end of the '90s
millennium looming and all that feverish excess

his bald head on the pillow
after chemo —

buddhist monk, baby, camp inmate.
He is sleeping.

I turn away quickly from that door into the room
that once was air above a green field
summer stitched through it by swallows' deft needlework

I turn away from that memory
coming down with the floodwaters

coming down on city and suburb alike.

Walking the riverbank early spring
I come upon a clean pool
deep and still and mirroring
each star, the new moon,
and my own shadowy face.

An epic for days, for long nights:
each breath he fought for and won.

After the hospital and his last breath
I walk out to the river;

always the river pulling down to the sea.

His last gift,
his last breath —
ripple on the pool
ripples out forever;

I watch him take it —
my first death.
My own breath on the mirror
rising mist on the river.

Hannah, Grandmother

for Hannah McCabe

Coldest day yet of November
her voice close in my ear —

tell them priests nothing.

Was I twelve? Thirteen?

Filthy minded.

Keep your sins to yourself.

Don't be giving them a thrill.

Dirty oul feckers.

As close as she came to the birds and the bees
on her knees in front of the Madonna,
Our Lady of the Facts of Life

beside the confessional —
oak door closing like a coffin lid

neatly carpentered
waxed and buffed.

In the well made box of this poem
her voice dies.

She closes her eyes

and lowers her brow to her joined hands.
Prays hard:

woman to woman.

A Remembrance of my Grandfather, Wattie, who Taught me to Read and Write

for Seamus Heaney

Heading towards the Natural History Museum
across the snowy paths of Merrion Square
the city hushed, the park deserted, in a daydream
I look up: a heaving net of branches, leaf-bare
against the pearly sky. There, like a trireme
on an opalescent ocean, or some creature of the upper air
come down to nest, a cargo with a forest meme,
only begotten of gall, of pulp, of page, of leaflight, of feather.
What snagged that book in the high reaches of the oak?
A child let out of school, casting heavenward the dreary yoke?
An eco-installation from an artist of the avant-garde?
Or the book's own deep need to be with kindred —
a rootling cradled again in grandfather's arms,
freed of her history, her spells, her runes, her fading charms?

Prayer for the Children of Longing

A poem commissioned by the community of Dublin's north inner city for the lighting of the Christmas tree in Buckingham Street, to remember their children who died from drug use.

Great tree from the far northern forest
Still rich with the sap of the forest
Here at the heart of winter
Here at the heart of the city

Grant us the clarity of ice
The comfort of snow
The cool memory of trees
Grant us the forest's silence
The snow's breathless quiet

For one moment to freeze
The scream, the siren, the knock on the door
The needle in its track
The knife in the back

In that silence let us hear
The song of the children of longing
In that silence let us catch
The breath of the children of longing

The echo of their voices through the city streets
The streets that defeated them
That brought them to their knees
The streets that couldn't shelter them
That spellbound them in alleyways
The streets that blew their minds
That led them astray, out of reach of our saving

The streets that gave them visions and dreams
That promised them everything
That delivered nothing

The streets that broke their backs
The streets that we brought them home to

Let their names be the wind through the branches
Let their names be the song of the river
Let their names be the holiest prayers

Under the starlight, under the moonlight
In the light of this tree

Here at the heart of winter
Here at the heart of the city

The Age of Reason

A garden, a privet hedge, the smell of fresh concrete.
A newly dug flower bed

is a black crescent moon

on a green sky.

       My Grandmother Mary
is picking lilac and roses to place on her May altar.

I think grace looks like the mother of pearl cover
on my eucharistic prayerbook,

Later a broken window, raised voices, my uncle
out of his head; all of us

sleeping in my auntie's bed.

Bad Fairy

The night of her christening:
the music blared, the cars and vans roared,
horns, sirens, beats,
all night, nobody could sleep.

There was a stabbing and a window got broken.
A car scratched with a key. One boy
got a bottle in the face
and someone puked in the garden.

I think of that now passing her house.
She must be all of nine
her face a shy moon
behind the twitching blind.

First Blood

A shadow cast by the clotheshorse onto the flickering wall.
heat of the fire, smell of scorched cotton.

Smoke, flame, alarm. Someone, my mother,
throwing the sheet into the fire.

My first sight of blood, her hand ripped on the fireguard.

Always after
a horse, a rider, a pointy-nosed devil,
riding the picture rail, the ceiling, the wardrobe,

coming to get us with fire, with blood.

When I Was a Girl

I longed for a boat
a hollowed log
seabirds carved its length
to fly it through the waves
of bleached white nappies in their rows

line after line
wave after wave
some sad celebration

for my setting forth

looking down on them through the big
window

Seán McDermott Street

22E Upper.

Shoes

The day I gave you back your death
I pulled off my winter boots.

Washed them. Waxed them. Polished them
Until I could see my shorn head

Grin back at me.
And though it was late November

And the snow was sifting quietly into drifts
In the pure light of the moon

I put on your summer shoes.
They smelt of the red red earth

Where lemons grow, where olives grow.
I walked away from the house.

The door swung shut behind me.

A Stray Dream

It's a happy dream though in it you were
Humping some dancer in a run down gaff

A seafront hotel out of season where
I'm in a kitchen on a single bed

I've pulled from a drawer like the silk scarf
Of the carny man who's filling in for

ManDuck The Magician star of stage and screen
I saw earlier that day at the end of the pier

I had sheets of Belfast linen but you
Had the dancer. And had her again

While the dawn struggled to break on the sea
And break on the quick and the slow and the dead

When I woke the next morning under the bed
Dustdevils, feathers and some child's brown shoes

Quitting the Bars

Quitting's hard but staying sober's harder.
The day by day; the drudge and boredom bit;
not sure if the self is cell or warder.

You quit the bars; you quit the sordid ardour;
you quit the tulpas sucking on your tit.
Quitting's hard but staying sober's harder.

You sometimes think you got away with murder.
The shady souls regard you as you sit —
you wonder if they are wards or warders

in this sad café. The mind's last border
dissolves. Guilt has done a midnight flit.
Quitting's hard but staying sober's harder.

So sip cool water; the light's a wonder
streaming out in wave-particles. You've lit
up bright your prison cell. Body — warder

of your dreams — will be the dreams' recorder,
though wrapped now in a skin that doesn't fit.
Quitting's hard but staying sober's harder;
stranger for your being both ward and warder.

Who'd be a dog?

Who'd be a dog, who'd be a poet's dog?
When we could be up the beach digging holes,
sniffing holes, cooling the paws in the sea,

she's stuck to her iBook, worrying a line
'stars so clear have been dead for years …
stars so dead have been clear for years …'
She thinks she's it with her buttons, her plug.

It's bye-bye puppy, hello Microsoft Word;
it's laptop now where once it was lapdog.

We look so cosy, me curled at her toes,
the two of us here in the house on our own.
If she dropped down dead this instant who'd know?
Who's a good doggy then, eh? Who's the best girl?

Give or take a day or two, it'd be a week max,
before, craven with hunger, I'd start in to eat:

top o' the foodchain to you, my last mistress!
as I lick at her bare, her coolèd feet.

Valentine

My sister phones to tell me that she found
when stripping old wallpaper from the hall
in thick black marker writ my name —
paula meehan kiss kiss love love — then yours,

enclosed within a heart. An arrow. The ground
shifts. I'd forgotten all that. I can call
to mind my nineteenth year with ease — the hames
we made of the job, woodchip (rough as furze

on the hands) overpainted green, the sound
of Dylan in mono, the rise and the fall
of your breath as you came and you went and you came,
as you did and you didn't, first mine, then hers,

then mine again. Never again. I'd sooner eat my
words, the wall they're written on. I'd sooner die.

A Change of Life

real danger. gambles. and the edge of death.
— from 'What You Should Know to be a Poet', Gary Snyder

PRAYER BEFORE STARTING

Let me just be
poised as that raindrop
on the tip of the tansy leaf
to freefall
to the earth below.

THE BOOK OF CHANGES

is best read by starlight
with plenty of time on your hands —
glint of coin, sheen of yarrow.

Elemental now, or mental
my two feet solid on this earth —
the path ahead, the path behind.

Not a question of which way to turn:
more a question of when to move —
the earth in its devotion carries all things

SCRYING

The stars have a purple glow and the red
devil of desire is jerking our strings:
we are avid puppets in his hands.

Enslaved by money and the lure of power
we rattle our talismans. Our dance,
if we have one anymore, is under

the baton of St Vitus, millennial, macabre.
This new fever has a grip on the island
and everyone wants, wants, wants

more space, more grace, more avoirdupois
wandering around with our lower material selves
hanging out — like that boy the other day

near the dying chestnuts at the station
who, shaking his penis at me, screamed
What are you looking at, witch?

SOLOMON'S SEAL

I am repotting in the front garden —
polygonatum multiflorum, aka St. Mary's Seal,
aka Sigillum Sanctae Mariae of the Lily family
which bears drooping tubular white flowers
in the axils of its broad sessile leaves.

I am dreaming its promise this autumn
of next summer's green wave
that will break over my ageing body.

A balm, a respite, this afternoon of
woodsmoke and drizzle and the days drawing in.

COMMON SENSE

A murmuration of starlings, a rowan tree.
Mid August berry feast
and berries raining down upon my head.

The music of what happens is
the sudden siren on the Coast Road
where the boy racer has hit the wall —
Coked up to the gills, says the cop —

and the brakes of the train pulling
into Bayside Station.
I'm walking the dog
by the dying grove of young chestnuts
where last year, maybe as a side line
to gathering conkers, children did
methodically strip each chestnut of its bark.

I wanted to wrap the trees in woolly jumpers —
those saplings shivering through the winter.
I watched them fail to bud and fail to leaf.

I watched them die through fair weather
through foul I have watched them die.
My beloved young chestnut grove.
And now an autumn without conkers!

We don't deserve this earth I sometimes think
and yet the children acted from ignorance.
I saw them at it: their rapt gazes as they stripped the bark
might have lent a renaissance artist faces for an altarpiece.

Common sense dictates there'll be bad luck
in store for them down their roads,
in dowry or in handsel they will fail
as the ballad has it.

            Nor would I wish to deal
the hand they have to play
or play it with them.

HECTIC

Walking the estuary today, Paula McCarthy,
passing the channel where I'd poured your ashes.
The two breasts of Howth beyond
to nestle your poor head against, my thought
five years ago, demented with grief.

I think of the scouring power of fire
in this the fire season, and of our last talk.
You were helping me move snails
from their lurking hides under the creeper
where they could nip (insofar as snails nip)
out in forays against my seedlings.

You asked about fire in Buddhism and what
it meant — you recalled a photo of a monk
burning in protest at the war.
Was there a Buddhist hell?

Only now. And now. And now — I joked.
And you laughed de profundis.
I don't remember what I said
But seriously ... some guff no doubt or
blah blah blah the way I do go on.

This autumn with the trees hectic in the woods
I'll let you drop leaf by leaf into the void,
let you leave drop by drop in the rain showers
let my love for you flower
in the far off fireworks of the city
as I lay my own demented head
on the two dun breasts of the hill of Howth to hear
as Yeats himself was wont to do when young
the eternal heartbeat of the mother.

We'll never know now what prompted you to use fire
and how much three weeks on Seroxat played its part.
Ourselves, we said, if come to that sad strait would
take some pills or score something lethal on the street
from Homer or Homeboy or whatyoumaycallhim
and nod off forever. As if one had a choice
in the matter. No mattter. We go on.

Foot before foot slog up the path.
O volcanic sister, O magma of sorrow,
O Roman candle, O meteorite shower,
O heavenly comet, O cut diamond,
O glint and gleam and shine,
Spark my obdurate heart.

The First Day of Winter

My head in the clouds
in the bowl of Akiko's
mother's white miso.

Single Room with Bath, Edinburgh

I slept last night in a room where someone died;
a narrow bed with polycotton sheets,
a window over wet deserted streets,
a tarnished mirror where my face was pied

and strange to me. I tossed, I turned; cold sweats
then prickly heat. I froze, I burned. I fell
into a dream that wasn't mine, some hell
hole, a smell of ether, legs open and wet

with blood. My own? Or the aborted near term child?
I could not tell. I felt my spirit ebb
and drift from me. For certain I was taking my last breath.

I heard a creature cry: part human, part wild.
It brought me to my senses, woke me to the web
of stars outside, refugee from someone else's death.

From Source to Sea

The light makes a river of the scars on your back.
I trace it from source to sea. It spills
off my page into silence, from the mouth into salt bitterness
of tears, beyond comfort of song or poem.

The light makes a river of the scars on your back.
I trace its course from neck to hip, its silken touch,
its pearly loveliness, its dream of shallows,
its song of pools, its memory of curlew
and nightingale, of heron and grebe.

The light makes a river of the scars on your back.
I walk the banks and pick for your pleasure
a posy of wildflowers, the smell of their names,
angelica, chamomile, calendula, dear vulneraries
with their balms and their powers, their beautiful petals
to soothe and to rescue, to help with the pain.

I trace the river the length of your back
to its source — a room, a house, a street
not unlike this one. A man is closing
the shutters on the light of morning. The same
light everywhere we rise to and greet.
He unbuttons his cuffs and rolls up his sleeves.
He is ready for work. So much to be done.

Etch

i.m. Osip Mandelstam

What was not committed to birch bark
was scribed in the memory of the hushed zeks
who took Osip's poem to heart.

His poem I write in my own breath
on the windowpane, the dear Irish rain
falling to the garden's purple vetch.

I'll spill acid on this plate
and fetch from deepest darkest shade
the lines that scarred the prisoner's face;

the light that struck in that most wretched place —
the wolves' tracking howl,
the birches singing out the forest's fate.

Troika

1. HOW I DISCOVERED RHYME

Not long back from London
my father had done a deal with a man
key money down on a house
in Bargy Road, East Wall,
an illegal corporation tenancy
in those days of no work, no roof,
no hope, no time like the present
to come home with three small children
and another on the way to what

was familiar at least. Dublin rain
and Dublin roads and Dublin streets
and Dublin pubs and Dublin pain.
Mayblossom in the park and empty pockets.

I think it was then my mother gave up:
pre-natal, post-natal who knows now.
They are so young, my mother and father,
to me who has grown old

in their light, in their shade.
They have too much on their plate —
including Ucker Hyland's chickens.
Part of the deal for the house
was to mind this man's chickens.
He kept them in the back yard
in makeshift crates and lofts.
Sporadically he'd deliver sacks of feed.
We'd have pots of popcorn every night
to Felix the Cat and to Bolek and Lolek
and the birthpangs of Irish Television.

We settled in. We fed the hens.
The man came. He took the eggs.
He'd wring the odd neck.
He wore two overcoats
belted by a length of rope.
And then a letter: the Eviction Notice.
Some neighbour had ratted us out.
There were rows, recriminations,
slammed doors, my father silent.

The stay in Bargy Road ended
on a bitter winter's day,
the Tolka low and the tang of rot.
We came home from school to bailiffs
boarding up the windows, to all
we had on show in the garden,
paltry in the dying light —
a few sticks of furniture,
the mattress with its shaming stain
nearly the shape of Ireland,
the Slot TV, our clothes in pillowcases
and our Christmas dolls grubby
and inadequate on the grass.

My mother was frantically chasing the chickens;
we put down our satchels and joined in.
My father was gone for the lend
of a van or a cart. The streetlights
came on and here comes
the henman around the corner —

Ucker Hyland! Ucker Hyland!
coats flapping and oaths spitting from his big lips
and all of us then round and round the garden
the winter stars come out and

feathers like some angelic benison
settling kindly on all that we owned.

2. A RELIABLE NARRATIVE

Why my maternal, and much feared uncle should visit
me now is a mystery. Both he and my mother dead,
me alone on the side of a mountain in Ikaria
a sanctuary sacred to a god of healing, Asklepius.

I was gathering herbs all morning, then sat
gazing out to sea in a half dream.
Hot springs with a sulphurous whiff,
the rocks around them a deep orange,
roil into the sea in a wraith of steam.

He comes *as large as life and twice as ugly.*
I put him down here in the hope he'll leave me be:
I must have brought him with me, packed
in my rucksack with Robert Graves' *The Greek Myths.*

I'm thirteen: my mother is sending me across the city
with Christmas presents for his children,
(all nine daughters — two sons he has yet to sire,
the only reason, he says, he has all those daughters,
trying for boys!)
                    I've to get
two buses with my parcels and the few bob for his wife
a dark beauty with sad eyes and many tired sighs.
We wouldn't have had that much ourselves
and I'm not to tell my father who's barred him

from the house, barred all mention of his name,
the way he'd turn up drunk and roaring.
We'd be under the covers shaking
or slipping out the back way to avoid him,
the way he'd pull our panties or pajamas down
and spit on our bottoms and rub the spit in.

Such a strange thing to do. I'll never fathom it.
I ask again what he meant by it in the shade
of this myrtle, in the thyme laden air
the salt taste of my own skin on my tongue.

Their house is a wreck when I get there —
windows smashed and boarded up.
Not a stick of furniture: orange crates to sit on
and jam jars for cups. So many children
with her beautiful eyes.
                              I'm queasy
in my brand new Christmas coat,
patterned with blue and green chevrons,
the first I've ever chosen for myself.
I want to leave that dark house
and run through that new estate
despite my squeaky shiny pinching shoes
to the bus and the city and the river and home.

I wonder even then how it all came to this:
when he arrives in spruced and groomed
in a mohair suit, rolling a fat cigar between thumb
and forefinger. The radio is playing Dickie Rock
or some similar contemporary pop.
We don't want to listen to this muck, he snaps it off
and takes me to the parlour which he keeps locked.
The only key.

Inside it's like a babby house
as the old ones used to say. All spic and span.
Carpeted. A three piece suite. A record player
long and slim, reminds me of a coffin
I saw a schoolmate laid out in.
And there in a cage a singing bird —
a canary by name Caruso. He takes him out
gently on a finger and strokes his yellow feathers.
He tells me he loves classical music
and he'll give me a fiver if I can name a classical composer.
I can and I don't. Nobody understands him
he tells me, especially not that cunt out there.
He smells of aftershave and stands too close to me.
He calls my mother a cunt too
and my father an ignorant fucker.

After nine daughters he got the sons he wanted.

His daughters grew to womanhood:
they taught their mother barring orders and legal separation.
They taught their mother the beautiful shining world
of work and peace and dignity and choice.
They taught their mother the new facts of life.

He outlived my own mother by thirty years.
He died alone one Christmas in a city centre flat.
His body lay there for days.

I lay him down now in the shade of a holm oak,
partridges chattering, late bees sipping still
at the wild mountain flowers. The sun is falling
behind the mountain, the Aegean turns blood red

for a moment, then fades to a pewter distance.
The moon is nearly full, stars are coming out
slowly, one by one, until the sky is a net
to catch me as I fall and fall and fall
further, willingly into its depths.

3. THIS IS NOT A CONFESSIONAL POEM

I write it in the light of ancient Greece
or in the ancient light of this mountain.
I write it in the shadow of the myths
or in the shadow of the people who made them.
I do not know that I've the right to say such things.
I only know I must.

I found her in the cold light of Finglas,
my mother curled to a foetal question
in the backyard. The stars were glittering
eyes in the night. The grass was rimed with frost
and crunched underfoot.
                    I remember
thinking how ill clad she was
for the night that was in it.
Her brushed nylon pajamas, her thin bare feet.
Ill shod. Not a sound to be heard
in the sleeping estate. Far off a dog.
Then another. A car starting up,
the engine having trouble catching.

I had woken from a dream of summer,
my first lover, to shouts and doors banging.
I had woken to my father calling out
my mother's name. Again and again.
And *dear sweet jesus* and *o christ.*

The downstairs windows were all open wide.
It brought the frosty air inside.
You could still smell gas.

I found her with her head in the oven.
I dragged her outside. Was all he said
then, and ever after. As if to allay accusation
or set his own story straight, or give the only facts
worth recording. He was not a man for elaborations.
Stoic? Or cynic? To this day I'm still in doubt.
Laconic for sure: though far from Ancient Sparta
he was reared, he would have fitted in.

We thought she was dead.
Her feet were like ice in my hands. Were
it not for the night that was in it
we might have missed her breath —
the thin reed of it rising, her sad tune to the air
proof positive she was still there.

We carried her in between us,
my father and I, never again that close,
or complicit. Never again the same as we were.

The doctor when she came was drunk
and worse than useless. Prescribed more
sleepers and downers, pocketed her fee
and stumbled towards her car.

The sun was coming up, the children
were whinging for their breakfasts.
The older ones were rushing off to school.

And that is how I leave them now:
I pull the door behind me firmly closed.

The past is a lonely country.
There are no charts, no maps.
All you read is hearsay, as remote
as the myths of this Greek island
where one small boat putters out to sea
in a blaze of morning sunlight
dragging my attention in its wake.

St. John and my Grandmother — an Ode

I am gazing out at Patmos where St. John
received the Book of the Apocalypse.
Some mornings it is on the horizon
very like the name the locals give it
boat of stone. Some mornings
you might see the monastery — a smudge
of white above the rock below the green
luxury of what shade there is, what shade
I imagine.
           More often it is hidden in a haze,
a rumour. What frightens me more
than his vision of the last days is the use
to which the holy book is put —
not content with its true worth, hallucinatory
dreamscape of the eternal now,
a highly polished mirror for the present times.
It's called the Word of God and that means trouble
for people like me. Always has. Always will.

It brings to mind my mother's mother Mary
who'd not an evangelical bone in her entire body,
loving, as she did, the way the earth was made.
All she asked was a decent crop of lilac
and roses coming in when the lilac'd fade.
To call her simple is to miss the point
entirely. Avatar of hearth mysteries,
true daughter of the moon, the shining one,
before she'd open the curtains of morning
whether winter or summer while the kettle boiled
she'd tell her dreams to her gathered daughters,
as apocalyptic in their cast as were St. John's.
She knew who died in the night,

who'd lose, who'd have a child.
The world was always signal portent,
every single thing stood for something else.
Her dreams, though I was not supposed to hear them,
could rivet, terrorize, warn or shrive you.
Her dreams were instruments of torture
for miscreant daughters who were out of line.
Her dream tongue my first access to poetry:
by her unwritten book I've lived, I'll die.
Here for instance is a dream she had of Marie
a younger daughter gone at seventeen
to work in nineteen fifties London, a scene
my grandmother can only imagine, having
never left Dublin : *Well, I got the boat
to Holyhead and then the train to Euston.
The tube then, the Northern Line
and there was not a sinner on it
but me and the driver, a blackman.
I got off at Angel, and came up to the street.
It was deserted. Not a sound but dead leaves
underfoot as if it was autumn. Brown
and gold and yellow and blood red the leaves
all the way to Marie's. I came to her door.
It was wide open. Marie, I called. Then louder,
Marie, Marie. Not a sound. I went in the door.
The house was all leaves underfoot,
all the way up the stairs. They were up to my knees.
Her bedroom door was open. I went inside.
Leaves up to my knees. I pushed across to her wardrobe.
I pulled the door open and what was before me
only Marie chopped in a hundred pieces, hacked to death.
And a river of blood came out of the wardrobe,
swept me in a wave right down the stairs
and out the front door onto the empty street.
Not a sound. Not a sinner.
Just leaves and blood. Leaves and blood.*

I sometimes tell this dream to my students
though it refuses a didactic read.
If they ask me where my poems come from
it's as good a place as any to begin:
Mary McCarthy's dream songs for her daughters,
as apocalyptic as the visions of St. John.
I heard them first before the age of reason.
They've stayed with me word for word
across half a century. I write one down now
in sight of Patmos, the island moving
like a trireme from me further into the haze
from which they both have come —
Mary McCarthy and the Evangelist John.

Hearth Lesson

Either phrase will bring it back —
money to burn, burning a hole in your pocket.

I am crouched by the fire
in the flat in Séan McDermott Street
while Zeus and Hera battle it out:

for his every thunderbolt
she had the killing glance;
she'll see his fancyman
and raise him the Cosmo Snooker Hall;
he'll see her 'the only way you get any
attention around here is if you neigh';
he'll raise her airs and graces
or the mental state of her siblings,
every last one of them.

I'm net, umpire, and court; most balls
are lobbed over my head.
Even then I can judge it's better
than brooding and silence and the particular hell of the unsaid,
of 'tell your mother...' 'ask your father...'.

Even then I can tell it was money,
the lack of it day after day,
at the root of the bitter words
but nothing prepared us one teatime
when he handed up his wages.

She straightened each rumpled pound note, then
a weariness come suddenly over her,
she threw the lot in the fire.

The flames were blue and pink and green,
a marvellous sight, an alchemical scene.

'It's not enough', she stated simply.
And we all knew it wasn't.

The flames sheered from cinder to chimney breast
like trapped exotic birds;
the shadows jumped floor to ceiling, and she'd
had the last, the astonishing, word.

The Mushroom Field

at the edge of the estate is gone now,
where I walked so many mornings
with my father before breakfast
in the autumn mist that wreathed the hawthorn

— That one morning when it started snowing
and we looked back at the tracks we had made.

I can hear them sizzling in the pan with butter
I can smell their otherworldly disdain,
and how they came on again and again.

I remember most the silence on those walks,
both of us lonely, both of us in pain.

There's a ten storey apartment block
and a shopping centre going in
over the traces of our footsteps,

the vestiges I lay down on this page
side by side, in the same rhythm, now;
making a path through autumn rain.

Archive

It is only when my father takes bad after Christmas
that we make the effort to get into his room.

It feels intrusive and yet it must be done
as delicately as we can we tiptoe round it.

With the sorting comes the weary recognition
that after this small room the earth shall claim him.

I sit amongst his things in the wintry sunlight
dusting, washing, swabbing down and with a shock

I recognize my younger rounder hand there
in sheafs of notes in tattered folders.

I turn a page and am restored to a Trinity classroom:
W.B. Stanford and the Roots of Greek Drama,

Dionysus and Beatlemania — an aside,
The Peloponnesian War, Pericles, the Athenian Fleet,

The Cynics, Stoics, Tyrants,
The Republic and Hesiod's *Works and Days.*

It's all I have to hold of my ancient confusions.
So much scattered in the squats and flats,

the vagaries of the road, the to's and fro's,
the wasted boys, those seasons down in hell.

There amongst my father's privacies
I forgive myself for the daughter I wasn't.

My Senior Freshman notes he deemed worth saving,
he who never spared a word of praise

or found a language of devotion except for horses.

My Brother Becomes a Man

on a particular October day. After the knock
on the door, after the first reports on the news.

I was in the kitchen in Eslin making bread
watching dough prove, stoking the range

listening to the same reports, oblivious;
thinking god help her she must have been

demented she must have been out of her mind.
The pictures in my head: a woman,

the seafront at Bray, a laneway, a hatchet, a child dead.
Never connecting. Never connecting to us.

When trouble comes to your door he
doesn't knock and he doesn't wipe his feet —

rugpulled tonofbricks punchinthegut no.
None of us were ever the same again.

But my brother who went to the morgue
and who gave the child back his name

who claimed him as one of our kin,
who placed him on the record of the State,

footnote to the times we are living in
as well as private pain, private fate,

my brother becomes a man there where he gazed
on the boy's dead face, when he took the image within

like a holy gift, an icon blazed in gold,
when he assumed the truth of the child's young soul

and shouldered it like the one true cross
and, man that he has become,

in silence he carries the weight and soldiers on.

The Wolf Tree

for Margaret Dorgan

To see the wolf tree is a skill best learned the hard way.
Or the easy way. So much depends on stillness.
Just look into the woods for as long as it takes:
the wolf tree is the one with laterals,
branches growing out and sideways from the bole.
You'll scan and scan and scan and fear
you can't find the tree for the woods
until the moment when your attention snags — a disruption
in patterning: horizontals suddenly when all around
are verticals. Once you find your first wolf tree
your vision will be sharper for the next, which may
also be hard to find. But never as hard as the first.

The wolf tree remembers when it was the only tree
in an open field. It remembers when
there was no competition for the light.
Because it had the field to itself it could be itself
in the wind and the rain and the blessed sun.
It is a kind of alpha tree, with a kind of alpha memory.

The trees that subsequently take root
from mast or nut or seed engendered, windborne
or carried on an animal's flank or shat down by birds,
these race towards the light and fight for it;
they reach straight upwards and mask the wolf tree
eventually, from all but the keenest loneliest eyes.

If you were to dream back through all the trees
in all the forests the earth has grown,
to the oldest, the original tree, the archaeopteris, say,

believed from a spore engendered,
and climb up through its ferny branches —
imagine the field you might survey,
imagine the vista that might unfold,
before the wolf tree's unleaving,
like the hours of your life,
finds you shivering, naked, unmasked and old:
revealed out in your own original domain
the desert sand moving towards you
the pressure mounting, the original diamond pain.

Coda: Payne's Grey

I am trying to paint rain

day after day
I go out into it

drizzle, shower, downpour

but not yet the exact
spring rain

warm and heavy and slow

each drop
distinct & perfect

that I wait for

by this water's edge
where some leaf of memory

will come down with the flood

the river in spate
broadening out to the sea.

from

Geomantic

(2016)

⁀

for Ciaran Carson and Deirdre Shannon

Indefatigable dazzling / terrestrial strangeness.
— Ciaran Carson

The Moons

Moons like petals adrift on the stream:
night moon and day moon, moon in eclipse,
slender new moon in the winter sky,
and full harvest moon — a golden ball;
moon of my first breath, my mother's death,
grandfather moon, my father's frail boat,
moon of my lost child, my sister's fall,
moon of my beloved's waking dream,
moons of my life adrift on the stream.

The Patternings

I sketch the patternings of the sea:
the iter- and reiteration
of event. Similar; not the same.

Lulled by dull predictability
of my own selves' dreary projections,
I've confused the sacred with its name.

Better scan fractals, rhyme sea with tree,
tune into tantric syncopation
my mortal gods, frantic and profane.

The Trust

Leave her in the lap of Our Lady —
her counsel for where to place the lost
when we close the door on their madness.
She slammed the door on her own daughter,
left her to the city's chartered streets,
found her in the Liffey's dark water,
cast up in the week before Christmas
the city gripped in the hardest frost
the eve of the new austerity.

The Conjuration

I walked your ghost trail through the city,
I knocked at all the old addresses,
but nowhere did I find word of you.
One friend said you'd died. It was a lie:
I knew by the shadows in her eyes.
She swore you'd been some class of a spy.
I was but one in a lengthening queue
of women crazed by your excesses,
fucking fools who deserved no pity.

The Rub

It was what she'd say when things got rough
back there in Thebes Central — the kitchen —
where it never came out in the wash,
the one original stain, the sin
of the fathers spun down through the years.
Every word she hurled could pierce the skin:
she could talk common, she could talk posh.
I sat like a stone growing lichen.
What didn't kill me would make me tough.

The Grimoire

When you call it my book of shadows
I scry the tawny deer move upwind
towards the Furry Glen, and the stars
above have their own kind of grammar,
their own declension of wingéd folk —
the Mother, the Father, the Other.
I understand the transit of Mars
is a fated course that has us twinned
lost souls beneath the skylight window.

The Row

No matter what you tell me tonight
about the lost republic, about
the last chance, the last hope, the last toss
of the coin, the flipside, the B side,
the be all and end all of nothing,
everything you say will be unsaid
by morning; and we've borne too much loss
between us to waste our breath in doubt
composing cruel censorious slights.

The Querant

There's nothing to be learned from the rain
falling through red, through green neon light,
nothing to be gleaned on the matter,

no solace in the sound of the train
shunting you home in the dark of night.
Under streetlamps the old boys gather

to talk of the old country, its pain.
Their childhoods dying in their hindsight,
with the smell of their fields in summer.

The Fear

Circling round the work for hours afraid
of what I might say or fail to say,
the song unmade, last night's dream betrayed,
I wander through the rooms: the rain,
which has drenched the unkempt streets for days,
beats a loud tattoo upon the pane
then stops of a sudden. The stanzas
open up to the sun's healing rays
answering my prayers — this mantra!

The Clouds

Some mornings the room is full of clouds,
clouds where the students' heads ought be,
little weather systems of their own.

They put all their work up on the cloud:
dream and song and secret and story.
Consciousness seeds the digital zone

with cold fronts, sunny spells, cirrus clouds.
Every weather of the room I grieve
the cloud children of the new machines.

The Last Lesson

Romantic, geomantic, antic:
the small green fields, the earth from above,
the autumn hedgerows, turning, turning,
turned with winter's white and black magic
into hieroglyphs of mortal love
signalling heaven with our yearning.
The frail glider suddenly mythic
is stopped a moment as if to prove
the craft is lighter than the learning.

The Feathers

To be so far up riding thermals
a summer's morning in early May
is to enter the realm of the hawk

or light born wingéd creature, angel
with a thunderclap come out to play
in the wave lift —
                    while below we walk

the sad road of the earthbound carnal
who dream flight, who scan the milky way
and turn the sky blue with crazy talk.

The Memory Stick

I searched high, low, all over the place
growing more anxious by the minute:
a whole summer's work in a square inch
cohesion of metal and plastic —
an ode, an elegy, a ballad,
a sonnet flawed by its rhetoric
but still retrievable at a pinch
if I could recall where I put it,
the memory stick in its shiny case.

The Fascinator

I tracked her through the marketplace by
the feathered contraption on her head.
She told me it was from the Latin
fascinare: to spellbind, or to cast
a spell, but I saw the rods, the axe,
the threads that bind us tight to the past.
Suddenly: early morning matins
drowning out the words best left unsaid,
minims rising to the empty sky.

The Pinhead

Just how many angels were dancing
last night in your junk dazed eyes? And how
in god's name, can you be such a drag

on this miraculous, entrancing
creation? You swear you can change now.
With your life in a black plastic bag:

we dread the sight of you — advancing
feathers flying, thunder on your brow,
frightening the children, and the dog.

The Spank

That time his grandmother sat me down
with sad news of a daughter's child
who'd turned to *spank* and who'd have thought it
of a boy so beautiful and smart?

Good family, everything to live for.

In the winter dusk, a heart to heart:
did I know where, from whom he bought it?
I'd seen him — sometimes meek, sometimes wild,
hustling for smack in his tarnished crown.

The Bird

O what can ail thee, little green bird,
singing your heart out this winter dawn?
From which suburban house have you fled,
plucky canary freed of your cage?
A murder of crows from the high pines
rejects your approach with raucous rage.
Gentle other, soon you'll be stone dead,
tangled feathers on the frosty lawn,
fallen angel in a fallen world.

The Gift

My godmother on her deathbed gave
up this memory of me aged two
in my grandmother Mary's garden
about the time I first got language.
Like a queen who rules all she surveys
I'm saying *nice nice nice* as I wave
to bee, fly, worm, wasp, bird, to the blue
cloudless sky, at home in creation,
my realm bordered by sweet privet hedge.

The Hide

This morning the white wash on the line
like prayer flags filling; then spilling
the wind onto the shadows below!

How thin, how vulnerable the skin
at wrist, temple, sole, throat, groin: the tongue
licks a secret path to the earlobe

and whispers to the creature within
the darkening words of an old song
while childhood ghosts buffet the window.

The Old Neighbourhood

I was dreaming of Gardiner Street
again, Georgian inner cityscape —
how they named it when they laid it out
somewhat like a natal horoscope,
squares that trine and sextile country seats.

As if summoned on some psychic Skype
the ghosts of my childhood manifest,
my feral girls, my angels, who skipt
summer into being with each beat.

The Boy from the Gloucester Diamond

What did we know of bogs? Their beauty?
The names of their flowers? Their wild skies?

We cursed those cold black-robed men who swept
the four winds and the four known seasons
out heaven's door down on us below.
They were beyond all sense, all reason.

By an unmarked grave we knelt and wept,
spoke of his head of curls, his green eyes,
his broken back. His small hands empty.

The Cardboard Suitcase

All he brought was his native city,
its jade green river, its streetsellers' cries,
hooves on cobbles, feral cats who crept
the grimy docks, old men with pigeons
whistling up winds, his granny's window,
the yard below, his mother's apron,
his sister's handbag — its smell. He slept
beyond reach of the fists, the lies.
He dreamt beyond reach of our pity.

The Understanding

I heard the kids in the back garden,
their grandfather's last day in the house,
his good blue suitcase parked in the hall.

—Da told Mr. Burke he's a goner:
  he's definitely not coming back home.

—Ma said he might if he gets better;
  he'll get lots of injections and all.

—Yeah right. It's like the place they sent Prince.
  It's where they put the old people down.

The Last Thing

my ebbing father said to me was
not the wind before he slipped below
the horizon of his morphine dream.

So was it the moon in the hospice
rigging? Or the cloud's buoyant shadow?
Or my mother's voice helming him home?

No. I think it was some ferocious
wingéd creature at the ward's window
breast feathers flecked with salt laced foam.

The Street

with only one tree was from a dream
of a city where I'd lost my mind
on a bright May morning that broken year,
and every soul passing my window

into the heart of their own mysteries

took a piece of me away with them,
their eyes confiding a double bind
that left me void, that tuned my ear
to woodwind in a summer hedgerow.

The Promise

I won't do it. Not today. I won't
do it, anyway. Not today. No.
Not because I can't do it. I won't.
Fallow fields lie dreaming under snow:
they won't be ploughed. Not this spring they won't.
On the fencepost, a grey hooded crow
is part of some mystery I won't
fathom now. Though I'm really quite low,
I won't do it. Not today. I won't.

The Syllables

Only the library angel knew
in which holy books the seeds were hid
that year they started cutting the tongues
out of the heads of the blasphemers.
One girl, a virgin, made a plain chant:
all those who heard took solace and drew
close; and we who can still speak are bid
sing it out at the top of our lungs,
seed syllables of the earth's dreamers.

The Poet

after Rilke

No beloved, no home to go to,
no place on this earth where I can stand
and call myself citizen. Alone
in the face of these days, these long nights,
each moment a bird that flies from me.
With empty hands I enter the light
of each creature, each flower, each stone;
my spirit incarnate bears the wound
of knowing, the price of making do.

The Moon Rose Over an Open Field

Count the syllables, a perfect line:
the way moon rises with the vowels,
the knacky way it moves on the tongue
and beats out its intent on the ear.
When I heard it first my fate was sealed:
it offered a pathway out of fear,
order from chaos when I was young,
a pure lyric from inchoate growls,
muse magic wrought from the power of nine.

The Godling

The downy ones over his breastbone
are the feathers I need to ruffle.
His fathomless eyes follow me round
the garden; he perches on my spade
and looks into the depths of the grave
I have patiently and neatly made.
He emits a sycophantic sound
striding through the morning's kerfuffle,
chiding me and my waning hormones.

The Melter

I remember you well in Grogan's.
You called it the Poet's Horror Hole.
And though it was easy to get there,
it was harder to find a way home.
Now that you're on the straight and narrow
with your charts, your mottoes, your slogans,
your strategies, your game plans, your goals
you're melting our heads with disasters,
with gossip, with lost-bar-god syndrome.

The Witch's Tit

that I was suckled at — those beestings
part Dublin, part Cork, wholly imbued
with notions of first and second place.

Who deserves a seat at the feastings?
Who gets leavings? Crumbs? Old bones well chewed?
I could never look her in the face,

tit for tat, without hearing these things:
pig, cunt, bitch, signal to her lewd,
kitschy, alcoholic fall from grace.

The Mother Tongue

Was it beaten into me or out
of me? Is it the lump in my throat
where words clot and snag and block the glut

that builds and builds and threatens to blow
my head off? Though there's no word for no,
grant me the words for grey hooded crow,

apple orchard, child, tenement, slut,
caravel, quinquireme, black sailed boat,
the far shining cities of the south.

The Poetry

Was it beaten into me or out
of me? The ur question, always doubt.

Never certainty, never sure the song
is on the right track. I've got it wrong

so often, failure is a true friend

of my long night's journey into day.
My gibbering ghosts must have their say:

Mother, Teacher, Lost Child, will not cease
until dawn breaks through in brutal peace.

The Book from Belfast

That day I thought I'd never find peace
or draw a sane breath this side of Hell,
the postman knocked with Berenson's tome:
Italian Painters of the Renaissance.
I couldn't read; typeface made me feel ill;
when I closed my sore eyes I would dream
witchsniffing burners from Aberdeen.
So then, your gift salvific — the grace
of childhood, all halo, wing, animal.

The Bonnet

That Samhain we dressed as characters
    from *Persuasion:* we gender-bended
through the Finglas fields. I wore velvet
    trousers and cravat. You pranced about
in a bonnet nicknamed Jane Austen:
    golden straw sprigged with silk columbine.

By the time we sat summer exams
    you were wasted. We read in your eyes
the opened grave, the funeral rain.

The Broken Bough

We held our breath when you were a boy
out on a limb of the old oak tree,
helpless below as you shimmied up
into its shadowy canopy.
That day the bough broke and you clung there
alone through the sudden thunderstorm.
We came upon you after unafraid
though drenched to the bone.

                          The pattern set:
all those times since, we wasted our breath.

The Lists

My list: candles, flowers, bulbs, butter,
a ream of copy paper, red pen,
red wine, something for Tracy's baby.

Your list: note for Johnny, note for Ma,
plastic sheeting, chair, six feet of rope.

I got the word in The Square, Tallaght,
by newborn layettes, pink and frilly,
your mother's voice sobbing down the line,
calling your name, over and over.

The Fever

Had I been sleeping I would have missed
the seagull at my sickbed window.
Just when I wondered was there something
stronger in the house to take away
my pain, I was lifted out of it
to soar above the square in the dark
on the seagull's salty myth flecked wings,
to navigate by stars, to follow
to the bitter end the fated tryst.

The Outbreak

I was by the fruit and vegetables
when I heard that war had broken out.

The vividity of a sudden
of all things in reach, in sight, in how

each upturned face was rendered sacred.

And in that moment I made a vow
that I would not let my heart harden

though all I valued be put to rout
by their betrayals, their reprisals.

The Luck

I don't do the past, said my father,
into my oldfashioned microphone.
The rain, the eternal Irish rain,
beats and beats and beats at the window
and the fattening geese are dreaming
of the north. I knew that he'd be dead
by Samhain when the geese returned again.
We bet online and watched the horses,
all going round the bend together.

The Pearl

My mother did nothing but the past,
over and over. Sifting the grains
for the one minuscule speck around
    which all of her grief accreted to pearl.
Historical grit — the first gunshot
    or first tricolour hoisted over
the G.P.O. that Easter lunchtime,
or a secret memory handed down
toxic in her lonely heart of hearts.

The Child I Was

Nineteen sixty six, eleven years
    old, let me die for Ireland I prayed,
Sword of Light in my grubby hand, though
    I thought the O'Connell Monument
was all about the wingéd women
    at its base, and when Nelson was blown
off his Pillar my Dublin sky wept.
    I understood we were poor — we lived
on streets named for the patriot dead.

The Commemorations Take Our Minds Off the Now

A boon to the Government; they rule
    in the knowledge that none can keep track
of just how much of the country has
been flogged like an old nag to within
an inch of its life. The karmic wheel
    goes round and round. I commemorate
the poor going round and round the bend.
    How mad do you have to be to make
sense of the state of the State we're in?

The Graves at Arbour Hill

We all die for Ireland in the end,
    whether sooner or later. I'll die
myself for Ireland one of the days.
    And even though I've lived for Ireland
with every breath of my being,
    with each and every beat of my heart
there'll come a day I'll be dust in wind,
    Irish dust in Irish wind, a hundred
and a hundred million years from now.

The Peace

Peace will come: let it begin with me.

Slogan from my wild and misspent youth,
comes back each time I practice Tai Chi,
when I meditate on the Seven,
    the Holy Seven Signatories.
I *Part the Horse's Mane,* I *Wave Hands
    Like Clouds,* I am a *White Crane Spreading
Her Wings.* When I *Grasp the Swallow's Tail,*
    I might undo the State's betrayal:
redemption through mastery of form.

The Clue

I don't do the past said my father
and turned back to his crossword puzzle:
three down 'sold out' eight letters — *betrayed*
'essential to life' five letters — *water*
'flag of the people'— *the starry plough.*

The seven stars on a field of blue —
dream of a republic, dream of hope.

Flowering on the island every spring,
stars and dreams: the natal horoscope.

The Singer

You are the gifted one, you are pure
joy in the morning early, you are
our broken hearts when night has come on
and the moon is full in the river
where the road winds down to the harbour:
a woman picks up a fountain pen
writes a farewell note to her lover,
a note she'll rewrite then abandon
before your canticle is over.

The Hands

Today I got my old woman's hands.
I laid my young woman's hands away
in the drawer with my young woman's hair,
that thick dark braid that hung to my waist.
Mind how he swung me once round and round
the garden, to Sergeant Pepper's Band.
That was long ago, a wedding day.
The ring is lost; lost are all my cares.
Old woman's hands now, old woman's face.

The Recipe

She believed it would strengthen the blood,
the soup my grandmother Mary made:
nettle, onion, parsley, thyme and spud —

each spring when the nettle tips appeared
in clumps the rough end of the back yard.
I, a willing and complicit ward,

dogged her footsteps. Thus to learn the hard
way what a nettle was, to learn that good
comes sleeved in pain, had best be suffered.

The May Altar, 58 Collins Avenue, Killester

You dressed it with lilac and privet,
the good crystal vase on white linen,
wax candles, bright medals, hymn singing
to Stella Maris, Star of the Sea.

You prayed to Our Lady to mind you.
You believed in angels and mercy.

As if heaven wept at your going
it rained the whole day you left Dublin,
rained on the girl you were, setting out.

The Offering

To kneel at the altar of memory,
to offer up what fragments we can
of the mystery that is your death.

Your life we are fated to carry
into each beautiful new morning
like emigrants safely come to land

after a rough crossing, their first breath
ashore — O sweet angel of mercy,
star of the wanderer, child of the sea.

The Beauty (Of It)

Northside graffiti of a morning,
acid colours along the train line,
suburban trippers out the window,

elders and the unemployed dreaming,
radiant in the winter sunshine
as if we believe both friend and foe

are tucked up safe from harm and sleeping
when we lift our eyes to the mountains
golden in their coverlet of snow.

The Web

i giorna della merla

I spun those nights to Van Morrison
on Fitzroy Avenue in a dream
part Victoriana, part nightmare.
Elsewhere, at my web's frayed selvage,
you were dying, less yourself each day
in a white cancer ward in Dublin.
I scanned your memory for this meme:
that time you talked me down, pulled me clear
of my fevered visions, my blank page.

The Great Poet

That strange full on proliferation
of verse after the great poet died,
as if a peerless diamond shattered
into smithereens and each facet
mirrored to infinity our dream
of perfect balance, integration.

We wrought newfangled order, implied
in patterns symmetric, then scattered:
fractals logarithmic and drastic.

The Age of Embrocations and Naps

can only be a matter of time:
this morning's blast of wintergreen
where once the scent of ylang ylang
permeated our chest of drawers.
A woman I hardly recognise
flits from mirror to mirror; older
and wiser, she speaks in a sing-song
voice which lulls us both to clearer dreams,
spooled snugly on her cold craft of rhyme.

The Old Professor

It's not just that he can't remember
you: he can't recall any of it —
the university, his other
students. I rocked. I reeled. I was knocked
off kilter, as if the child in me
had stepped up to the blackboard and picked
up the chalky duster and wiped her
future lines away, even the bit
where he helps me get sober and clear.

The January Bee

who comes to the winter flowering shrub,
grief in his empty pouches, who sups
alone in the stilled garden this dusk:

I would have missed him only I stopped
mid-argument to catch the moonrise
over the wet roofs of the suburb

and caught him at work deep in the musk,
shaking the bells of the scarce blossoms,
tolling our angers, ringing in peace.

The Hexagram

Before starting find the lines — broken
and whole — arranged as a hexagram;
the crescent moon waxing, a token

in the night sky of beginnings. Palms
open to the grace of what might fall
like snow to the snow-white page. How calm

I am, and cool, when I hear the call.
She has found me out, in my silence,
come with rumours of heaven, of hell.

The Struggle

In my garden — teasel, nettle, thistle,
taken hold since I lifted my hand;
with thorn, sting, clawed hooks they do battle

bristling towards the ruin of my house.
Like poetry — territorial
and patient. Humble only to bees;

flowering to them, opening to them,
and how, against winter's unleaved trees,
they scribe gracenote, quaver, minim.

The Thaw

I watch a she wolf treading thin ice
beyond the birches. I hold my breath —
muffled river music. Lost balance

and the wolf stumbles, skirts death,
jumps to the bank just as the ice cracks,
her shadow snagged by water. Beneath

the trees, snowdrops measure the exact
shift in light that ends the long winter —
and out there on the snowfield her tracks.

The Leningrad Muse

What cracked the ice, what broke the silence?
Groans of prisoners. After thunder,
church bells pealing. Out of the violence

her voice clear above mocking laughter.
Flute music then and her frantic dance;
on the east wind news of fresh torture.

Drumbeat. Heartbeat. Edge of edge of chance.
She moves through me: mother and daughter,
ancient lover. She works me to trance.

The Line

I find the line. I lose it. I find
the line again. I turn it over
and feel it move through ear, heart, mind,

tracking the prints back to the haunt's mouth
beside a frozen lake, beneath trees
where again I'm fated to give birth.

Blood on my tongue, her pelt licked and eased
from nose to tip of tail. The black earth
under snow yearning for tender green.

The New Regime

After love we sleep curled together.
I am dreaming her old dreams; she dreams
pines freighted with snow, ice storm weather.

Her mouth's rimed with my milk, her hair streams
in curls and rivulets down her back.
She is spelling out the new regime —

its ins, its outs, my place in the pack;
where she keeps the names of the lost things.
how to bear the pain, the sweats, the rack.

The Withdrawal

Strung out again I stumble through nights
without her. Cold grey street. Hot grey sheet.
Body drab as lead I shun the light.

She has shown me what it's like to die.
Bereft, out of favour, I won't write
one syllable of truth, one good lie.

I crave her cool comfort, her deep shade.
She's busy elsewhere despite how I try
to lure her back with this song I've made.

The Hempen Rope

And thus I turn what she has given.
I offer it up to them in hope,
in despair, part wasted, part shriven,

I have twisted my own hempen rope
with those sad listeners as witness.
Though I know nothing of how they cope

in their real, their secret lives, I bless
them in their every generation
in their devotions, in their duress.

The Contract

From the fret of insomnia some
cold lines on a page; a candle
gutters on the windowsill. Oh come

morning bells, call me back to myself,
call sinner and saint to watch snow fall
on the city, the forest, the wolf

tracking her pup the length of the lake.
Before this moon clears the horizon
I'll give whatever she needs to take.

The Poem for Dillon with North Carolina in It

After the slammed doors the door opening
to my broken face; and the window
that gave onto darkness engulfing
your humid subtropical biome.
Red fox and red wolf and white tailed deer.
Cornsnake, milksnake, diamond back rattler,
the copperhead you taught me to fear —
they slither through memory's field: rare,
heraldic, set now and fixed in print.

The Black Kite

the children fly over Burrow Beach
this August morning

— (like the black sails
Aegeus saw bearing on Athens
portending grief and the fall of his house,
or like Victorian widows' weeds,
an incongruity of black bows) —

which by a sudden squall is taken
struggling out to sea. When it fails
and falls, it falls far beyond our reach

The Ghost Song

'The singers and workers that never handled the air'
— Gwendolyn Brooks

From a dream of summer, of absinthe,
I woke to winter. Carol singers
decked the walls of some long lost homeland,
late night shoppers and drowsy workers
headed for the train.
                            So the night that
you died was two faced, June light never
far from mind though snow fell. I handled
grief like molten sunshine, learned to breathe
your high lithe ghost song from thinnest air.

The Inscription

'Honour the dust ...' wrote Gary Snyder
in my old copy of *No Nature*
before Bella, our beloved dog,
got her teeth into it. Now dog eared,
well chewed, much annotated, it sits
on a bockety shelf right beside
the well made box wherein lies her wag,
her bark, her growl, her lick, her rapture
of devotion — her dust we honour.

The Storm

When we first met the hedgerows were white
with blackthorn blossom. Nineteen ninety:
the February storm that brought down

the ancient oaks and shook the rafters,
that grounded planes, that closed all the ports,
picked us up and threw us together.

Like refugees newly come to town
we made a stern language of beauty
all spring into the summer's stretched light.

The Blues

In moonlight the landscape was all blue —
frit of cobalt, French ultramarine,
far off hills of phtalocyanine
and that gleam of light on lake water
cerulean, shore rocks indigo,
fugitive soldiers freezing to death
on a Prussian ground — when my beloved
turned on me his eyes of blue mercy:
lapis lazuli, pupils of gold.

The Flood

It was only when it receded
we knew it for the gift it had been.
If truth be told we missed the water.

It was exactly what we'd needed.
We missed the way it made a mirror —
doubled goose, godwit, egret, heron;

and that once in moonlight we looked down
on two complete and drowning strangers,
those depths where later wolfbane seeded.

The Woodpile

We worked our way through it log by log:
three winter's worth of heat, precious light
through the darkest nights, the darkest days.

You'd remarked you knew the very tree,
that last June you stacked them in the barn —
the silver logs in their fret of moss.

You must have had the news already
whistling from the woodpile's finished height
your arms about your favoured black dog.

The Quilt

It was a simple affair — nine squares
by nine squares, blue on green —spots, stripes, bows
alternate with gold on red chevrons:
my grandmother's quilt I slept under
the long and winding nights of childhood.

Above the bed a roundy window:
my own full moon. I loved the weathers
wheeling past, the stars, the summer suns;
my aunties' deep breaths, distant thunder.

The Food Chain

I could eat the moon, the breaking waves,
the moonlight sifting through the pine trees;
I could eat you, my beauty, your gaze

following that scrawny village cat
who stalks the plump frog who stalks the bug
who labours over the hessian mat

while we eat little silver fishes
and are nibbled on in turn by flies
glazed by the shine of this blood moon's rise.

The Road to Agios Kirikos

I imagine our ghosts hand in hand,
the full May moon overhead, the smell
of oregano, of thyme, of sage;

I imagine they'll pause at the wall
where the glow worms between the stones
sing the stardust of which they're made.

They can ramble at their ease, they've all
the time in the world before the day
claims, from their bright souls, their dying minds.

The Handful of Earth

Under scrutiny it tells us all
we need to know about our futures
it being composted of our past lives,
the nine years in this house by the sea.
Under the paths stars make, wild birds call.

I fancy I could read it like leaves
of tea, yarrow stalks thrown down, tarot,
its minutest narratives of grief
its aboriginal patternings.

The Sea Cave

It is as close as I'll get to her
in this life: to swim into the dark
deep in the cave where the hot springs are,

to float in her amniotic dream
of children, of a husband, of home.
Flickers of light there where minnows teem

like memories pulsing through my veins,
that lull me, that shrive me, uncertain
whether I hear her heartbeat or mine.

The Island

At home again on Ikaria,
our own bee loud glade. How this morning
hawks were hung in the still mountain air;
a snake slithered into the kitchen,
three elegant feet of fear; the cats,
those thin village cats, napped in sunlight;
and last night's owl, startled into flight
has us unsettled and creaturely
ourselves, sweeping the sea-girt garden.

Acknowledgements

Gratitude to the many editors, directors, curators, broadcasters, anthologists, film makers, musicians, dancers and fellow poets who helped bring these works to fruition. Gratitude to the judges and estimators who gave me awards, and to those who gave me resources to buy the time to make the poems. Gratitude to the Arts Council / An Chomhairle Ealaíon for early support and to Aosdána for the honour and for the Cnuas.

Gratitude to Pat Boran & Raffaela Tranchino, AKA Dedalus Press for this opportunity to select and republish the poems from five collections originally published during the years 1990 to 2016. Gratitude to Michael Schmidt, for his help with the two volumes *Dharmakaya* and *Painting Rain*.

Gratitude and love to my siblings, to whom this book is dedicated, and to the wider circle of family and friends who have nourished me in so many ways.

Gratitude to my teachers, especially to James J. McAuley who helped me put the poems under the kind of pressure that advanced me as an artist.

Last, but not least, three deep bows of gratitude to my beloved companion, Theo Dorgan.

Lightning Source UK Ltd.
Milton Keynes UK
UKHW041838021120
372676UK00001B/62